Daniel Giraud Elliot

The Gallinaceous Game Birds of North America,

including the partridges, grouse, ptarmigan, and wild turkeys

Daniel Giraud Elliot

The Gallinaceous Game Birds of North America,
including the partridges, grouse, ptarmigan, and wild turkeys

ISBN/EAN: 9783337289126

Printed in Europe, USA, Canada, Australia, Japan

Cover: Foto ©Andreas Hilbeck / pixelio.de

More available books at **www.hansebooks.com**

THE
GALLINACEOUS
GAME BIRDS

OF

NORTH AMERICA

INCLUDING THE PARTRIDGES, GROUSE, PTARMIGAN,
AND WILD TURKEYS; WITH ACCOUNTS OF THEIR DIS-
PERSION, HABITS, NESTING, ETC., AND FULL DESCRIP-
TIONS OF THE PLUMAGE OF BOTH ADULT AND YOUNG, TO-
GETHER WITH THEIR POPULAR AND SCIENTIFIC NAMES

*A book written both for those who love to seek these birds afield with
dog and gun, as well as those who may only desire to learn the
ways of such attractive creatures in their haunts*

BY

DANIEL GIRAUD ELLIOT, F. R. S. E., ETC.

Ex-President of the American Ornithologists' Union
*Author of the "New and Heretofore Unfigured Birds of North America,"
of the "North American Shore Birds," of the Illustrated Mono-
graphs of the Ant Thrushes, Grouse Pheasants,
Birds of Paradise, Hornbills, Cats, etc.*

WITH FORTY-SIX PLATES

SECOND EDITION

NEW YORK
FRANCIS P. HARPER
1897

PREFACE.

No group of animals is more important to man than the one comprising the gallinaceous birds—the source from which has been derived the countless varieties of domesticated fowl distributed throughout the world.

As articles of food they are of inestimable value, and the birds enter largely into the various accounts of trade. But beside the commercial aspect, which is important enough, the species present other attractions that appeal most strongly to those for whom this book was especially written, the sportsmen—viz., the pleasure they yield in the chase, and the incentive they provide for action and effort, when, in the leafy aisles of the whispering forests, or in the thickets, and along the banks of the leaping stream, or on the open sky-encircled prairie, man in his quest for these game-like creatures, aided by his faithful dog, finds renewed health and strength to wrestle with the toils and troubles of his daily life. For accomplishing this result alone, even if in all their life and death they yielded no other, these birds were not created in vain.

The favorable reception given to my book on the "Shore Birds" has encouraged me to write the life histories (as my opportunities have enabled me to become familiar with them) of possibly the most attractive feathered creatures, certainly so from the sportsman's point of view, which our country possesses. The water fowl to some may appear more desirable, a few are really game, and I would be the last to speak or write disparagingly

of them; but the environment of the Ducks and Geese
suffers in comparison with that of gallinaceous birds,
and the beautiful pictures of high-bred dogs, seeking and
pointing game, are lacking in the pursuit of the web-
footed quarry.

The construction of the present volume is precisely
similar to that of the "Shore Birds," and first is given
the common name of each bird, or, if there are more than
one, that most generally employed. Then follows an
account of the habits and economy of the species, and
a short life history; after which comes the Latin name
succeeded by the geographical distribution, and a description of both sexes when necessary, and of the young
whenever possible.

In the Appendix will be found the Keys to the Families,
Subfamilies, Genera, and Species, arranged in the same
simple manner as those published in the "Shore Birds,"
and which will enable anyone with a little patience to
ascertain to what species an unfamiliar example may
belong. Excepting perhaps the Ptarmigan, the various
species of gallinaceous birds are more easily recognized
from each other, in illustrations printed only in black and
white, than are those of the "Shore Birds," and the
various Keys will be found perhaps less necessary, and
only really required in the cases of the group above mentioned, or in closely allied species of Prairie Grouse.

The author's experience among the game birds has
been very extensive, gained from a familiar acquaintance
with them in their haunts extending over many years.
With a few exceptions, he has observed all the species
contained in this book in the various localities they frequent throughout North America, and in the proper
season representatives of most of them have fallen to his
gun. Unlike the majority of the "Shore Birds," omit-

ting a few species and those mainly among the Ptarmigan, Partridges and Grouse breed within the limits of the United States, and their habits in the nesting season can be observed by anyone who may be sufficiently interested to visit those parts of our country in which the birds are to be found.

Their nests are similar in construction, but the eggs vary greatly in coloration, and some, like those of the Ptarmigan, are strongly characteristic and unmistakable in their markings. The eggs of the Partridges are usually of one color and unspotted, those of the Grouse and Turkeys more or less covered with spots, which differ in hue from the ground color.

Having provided in the work on "Shore Birds" a map which gave the position and name of all the different portions of a bird's plumage, it does not seem necessary to issue another for the birds contained in this, a companion volume, for the arrangement of the plumage in all birds is the same, although the shape of the feathers may be very different, and the terms by which these are known do not vary.

The plates which adorn the volume are the production of the clever pencil of Mr. Edwin Sheppard, who illustrated the "Shore Birds," and like those drawings, these, executed with equal fidelity, will be of the utmost assistance in helping those unfamiliar with the species to recognize their specimens without difficulty.

The Latin names employed, except when reasons are given in the articles or in the Appendix for changing them, are those of the last edition of the Check List issued by the American Ornithologists' Union.

The author sincerely trusts that this book will prove to be of value to all sportsmen, and help bring to their memories halcyon days amid the game birds in tangled brake or open prairie, and that the student, desirous of learning the ways of life and variations in dress of one of the most gallant and attractive groups of birds living to-day, may, find some profit and instruction in a perusal of its pages.

My thanks are due to my friends Professor Allen and Mr. Chapman of the New York Museum of Natural History, to Mr. R. Ridgway of the Smithsonian Institution, and to Mr. Whitmer Stone of the Academy of Natural Sciences of Philadelphia, for the loan of specimens of the various species from which the illustrations in this volume have been made.

TABLE OF CONTENTS.

	PAGE
PREFACE,	V
LIST OF ILLUSTRATIONS,	xi
INTRODUCTION,	xiii
BOB WHITE,	19
THE FLORIDA BOB WHITE,	32
TEXAN BOB WHITE,	35
MASKED BOB WHITE,	38
MOUNTAIN PARTRIDGE,	41
PLUMED PARTRIDGE,	44
SAN PEDRO PARTRIDGE,	47
SCALED PARTRIDGE,	49
CHESTNUT-BELLIED SCALED PARTRIDGE,	53
CALIFORNIA PARTRIDGE,	55
VALLEY PARTRIDGE,	58
GAMBEL'S PARTRIDGE,	62
MASSENA PARTRIDGE,	69
RUFFED GROUSE,	74
OREGON, OR SABINE'S GROUSE,	81
CANADIAN RUFFED GROUSE,	84
GRAY RUFFED GROUSE,	88
DUSKY GROUSE,	90
SOOTY GROUSE,	94
RICHARDSON'S GROUSE,	98
CANADA GROUSE,	100
FRANKLIN'S GROUSE,	106
PRAIRIE HEN,	110

	PAGE
Heath Hen, . . .	117
Lesser Prairie Hen, .	120
Attwater's Prairie Hen,	122
Sharp-Tailed Grouse, . .	123
Columbian Sharp-Tailed Grouse,	126
Prairie Sharp-Tailed Grouse, .	129
Sage Grouse, .	136
Willow Ptarmigan,	142
Allen's Ptarmigan,	149
Rock Ptarmigan, .	151
Reinhardt's Ptarmigan,	154
Welch's Ptarmigan,	157
Nelson's Ptarmigan, .	159
Turner's Ptarmigan,	161
Townsend's Ptarmigan,	163
Evermann's Ptarmigan,	165
White-Tailed Ptarmigan,	167
Wild Turkey, . .	172
Florida Wild Turkey, .	177
Elliot's Rio Grande Turkey,	180
Mexican Turkey, .	182
Appendix,	189
Index, .	213

LIST OF ILLUSTRATIONS.

1. BOB WHITE, ... *Frontispiece*
2. FLORIDA BOB WHITE, *Opposite page* 32
3. TEXAN BOB WHITE, " " 35
4. MASKED BOB WHITE, " " 38
5. MOUNTAIN PARTRIDGE, " " 41
6. PLUMED PARTRIDGE, " " 44
7. SAN PEDRO PARTRIDGE, " " 47
8. SCALED PARTRIDGE, . . . " " 49
9. CHESTNUT-BELLIED SCALED PARTRIDGE, " " 53
10. CALIFORNIA PARTRIDGE, " " 55
11. VALLEY PARTRIDGE, " " 58
12. GAMBEL'S PARTRIDGE, " " 62
13. MASSENA PARTRIDGE, " " 69
14. RUFFED GROUSE, ... " " 74
15. OREGON, OR SABINE'S RUFFED GROUSE, " " 81
16. CANADIAN RUFFED GROUSE, " " 84
17. GRAY RUFFED GROUSE, . " " 88
18. DUSKY GROUSE, " " 90
19. SOOTY GROUSE, . " " 94
20. RICHARDSON'S GROUSE, " " 98
21. CANADA GROUSE, " " 100
22. FRANKLIN'S GROUSE, " " 106
23. PRAIRIE HEN, " " 110
24. HEATH HEN, . " " 117
25. LESSER PRAIRIE HEN, " " 120
26. ATTWATER'S PRAIRIE HEN, " " 122

27. SHARP-TAILED GROUSE,   .   .   *Opposite page* 123

28. COLUMBIAN SHARP-TAILED GROUSE,   "   "   126

29. PRAIRIE SHARP-TAILED GROUSE,   "   "   129

30. SAGE GROUSE,   .   "   "   136

31. WILLOW PTARMIGAN,   .   .   "   "   142

32. WILLOW PTARMIGAN IN WINTER,   "   "   146

33. ROCK PTARMIGAN,   .   "   "   151

34. ROCK PTARMIGAN IN WINTER,   "   "   152

35. REINHARDT'S PTARMIGAN,   "   "   154

36. WELCH'S PTARMIGAN, .   "   "   157

37. NELSON'S PTARMIGAN,   "   "   159

38. TURNER'S PTARMIGAN,   "   "   161

39. TOWNSEND'S PTARMIGAN,   "   "   163

40. EVERMANN'S PTARMIGAN,   "   "   165

41. WHITE-TAILED PTARMIGAN,   .   .   "   "   167

42. WHITE-TAILED PTARMIGAN IN WINTER,   "   "   170

43. WILD TURKEY,   .   "   "   172

44. FLORIDA WILD TURKEY,   .   "   "   177

45. ELLIOT'S RIO GRANDE TURKEY,   .   "   "   180

46. MEXICAN TURKEY, ... "   "   182

COLOR CHART AT END OF THE VOLUME.

INTRODUCTION.

THE great division of the Class Aves called GALLINÆ, sometimes designated RASORES (*Latin rasor, a scraper*), from the habit possessed by its members of scratching the ground in search of food, is composed of two suborders and four families. Of the latter we have to do at the present time with only two—TETRAONIDÆ and PHASIANIDÆ, containing those species which have *fowl-feet*, in contradistinction to the other two families—MEGAPODIDÆ and CRACIDÆ, which have feet like a pigeon.

These four families comprise between three and four hundred species, distributed throughout the world, and are of the very highest importance in their relation to man, affording food to multitudes of people, and the members of the PHASIANIDÆ are the sources of all the domesticated poultry found in the world to-day.

In form the birds are usually heavy in body with rather stout legs and feet, small heads and curved bills, with the nostrils placed in a membrane covered by a scale, and the wings are short and rounded. In some subfamilies the males, and occasionally the females, have the legs armed with spurs, and certain species have several spurs at a time upon each leg. The sternum, or breastbone, has a double bifurcation on each side, the fissures wide and deep, and provides but little space for the attachment of the great pectoral muscles, which however are well developed, and give the plump appearance to the breast so characteristic of these birds. The tail is of various shapes, and in the PHASIANIDÆ is sometimes lengthened enormously, and occasionally the feathers are highly decorated by various markings or brilliant coloration. The flight is labored but rapid, and occasionally protracted.

In their anatomy these birds have various peculiarities. The esophagus is dilated, forming the crop which receives and moistens the food; while the gizzard, which is present in all save the Sage Cock, is very strong, with a thick, hard, interior wall. To assist this organ in grinding the food the birds are in the habit of swallowing small stones and other hard objects. The cœca are highly developed.

The species of this order are accustomed to lay numerous eggs, to go in coveys of considerable numbers, composed at times of one or more families, and the young, which are at first covered with down, are able to run and feed as soon as hatched. The family TETRAONIDÆ, which comprises the great majority of gallinaceous birds inhabiting North America, contains those known as Quails, Partridges, and Grouse, and is represented in every portion of the world. The members differ greatly from each other in many particulars, and form three rather natural groups or subfamilies, one of which, the Perdicinæ, or Old World Quails and Partridges, are not found upon the Western Hemisphere. American Partridges have certain peculiarities, more particularly described in the Appendix, which place them apart and distinguish them from their relatives across the sea, while certain species of Grouse have so wide a distribution, retaining at the same time their specific characters, that they are found in high latitudes throughout the world. This can be said of but very few species of birds known to ornithologists at the present day.

The three subfamilies—PERDICINÆ, ODONTOPHO-
RINÆ, and TETRAONINÆ—comprising the family TE-
TRAONIDÆ, are known in ornithological language as the
Alectoropodous (Greek ἀλέκτωρ, alector, a cock + πούσ,
pous, a foot) Gallinæ, or, to translate it freely, fowl-
footed gallinaceous birds, characterized by having the
hind toe raised above the plane of the front toes and clear
of the ground; differing in this respect from the other
section of the order, the pigeon-footed gallinaceous birds,
or Peristeropodous (Greek περιστερά, peristera, a pigeon,
+ πούσ, pous, a foot) Gallinæ, which have the four toes
resting on the ground, all on an equal plane. The
Grouse are distinguished from all members of the order
by having the tarsus, or shank, covered with feathers
more or less completely, sometimes even the toes are
hidden, resembling in this respect certain rapacious
birds, such as Owls and a few species of Hawks and
Eagles. As they are mostly inhabitants of countries
where the winters are usually long and severe, this provision of nature affords additional and especial protection against the cold, and guards those parts that are
particularly exposed from the danger of becoming frozen
and probably lost or rendered useless.

The members of the subfamily TETRAONINÆ have
many characters that distingush them from other birds,
not the least of which is the gracefully shaped and thoroughly game-like head, high in the rear, or occipital
region, with a broad and ample brain case, sloping gradually forward and contracting toward the junction with the
curved and usually powerful bill. The brain is large for
the size of the birds, and it bestows upon them unusual
intelligence, as shown in their cunning, ability to adapt
themselves to their surroundings, and fertility of resources in avoiding danger. A Quail, Grouse, or Tur-

key is far from being a stupid bird, and even man, with his wisdom and variety of methods, has often need of all his wits to circumvent these wide-awake feathered creatures.

Gallinaceous birds are terrestrial, but none of them will hesitate to fly into a tree and walk or roost on the branches, and they frequently seek the cover of the foliage when pursued, for protection and concealment. They are apparently perfectly at home upon a branch, fence, or similar support, their rather long toes grasping firmly the perch on which they have taken their position.

Grouse and Turkeys are generally polygamous, but the Odontophorinæ, or Partridges, are monogamous. The females of those addicted to the former practice are usually in the habit of concealing their nests not only from their natural enemies, but also from the males, some of which would destroy both eggs and young if they found the opportunity. In the other class the male is assiduous in his attentions to his mate when engaged in the duties of incubation, not infrequently relieving her by covering the eggs himself, and always shares in caring for and feeding the young. It is a rather singular fact that in most polygamous species the plumage of the sexes is very dissimilar, while there is usually but little difference observable between those that are monogamous. As a rule the birds contained in this volume moult once a year in the spring before the commencement of the breeding season, but the Ptarmigan are an exception, and are in a continuous state of moult at all seasons, except, possibly, for a very brief period after they have assumed the breeding dress, and again in winter when robed in white. All Ptarmigan turn white in winter, excepting the Scotch Grouse, so called, which, possibly from the effects peculiar to its insular habitat, retains a plumage of the same colors throughout the year. This provision of nature for the other species, may be to give an additional security to the birds when the whole country of their northern homes is covered by snow, and so assimilate them to the surrounding whiteness, that their presence can only be perceived with great difficulty or by merest chance.

Many Grouse possess a peculiar structure, rarely found in any other species, in the air sac on the side of the neck which is capable of being inflated, and then resembles somewhat an orange attached to the neck. By exhausting the air, which can be accomplished at the will of the bird, a booming sound is produced that may be heard at a great distance. This performance usually takes place at the breeding season, and is one of the male's allurements to secure the attention and probable fleeting attachment of the females. At all other seasons this sac shrivels up and is mostly concealed under the feathers.

One species of another group—Shore Birds—possesses a similar sac, but differently disposed and of great extent, which is also exhibited to advantage during the breeding season. This is the Pectoral Sandpiper, a description of whose performance on the tundras of the far north I have given in my work on the *Limicolæ*.

North America has been most favored among the countries of the earth in the great variety and number of her gallinaceous birds, many of the species being equal to any found in other lands and some surpassing all others known, in size, magnificent appearance, and in their value, commercially and otherwise, to the human race. They are a precious heritage, to be guarded carefully and used judiciously if we are wise and far-seeing,

bestowing benefits on ourselves and on succeeding generations, or to be recklessly squandered like the fortune
of the spendthrift, leaving to posterity not even a
memory, but simply a tradition of the noblest race of
feathered creatures Nature ever produced. Which shall
it be?

GAME BIRDS OF NORTH AMERICA.

BOB WHITE.

WIDELY distributed throughout the Eastern portions of the United States, from southern Ontario on the north to Florida on the south, this most attractive little bird, called in the Northern and Middle States Quail, and in the South Partridge, is the best known and most eagerly sought of all our game birds by the lovers of dog and gun who rejoice in the sports of woods and fields. It is a sociable species, frequents cultivated lands, resorts to the vicinity of the farmer's dwelling and barns, and follows the onward march of the pioneer as he penetrates the wilderness to conquer the rough places of the land, and produce smiling sunlit fields where once the darkening forests stood. In Vermont, New Hampshire, and northern New York it is rare, and occasionally occurs in Maine, but throughout the Eastern States, except Florida, and west of the Mississippi in the States of Missouri, Kansas, Arkansas, Louisiana, eastern Texas, northern New Mexico, and the Indian Territory it is more or less abundant; and is steadily advancing westward in the track of the new settlements and cultivated land.

It has been introduced into South Dakota, possibly from Florida, as the birds I have seen from that far Western State resemble very closely those from the southern peninsula, and in 1871 some were turned loose in the Great Salt Lake Valley, Utah, and are now common in various portions of that State. In 1875 a few were liberated at Boisé City, Idaho, and not many years after the birds were numerous along the Boisé River and west of the Snake River. It has also been introduced into Colorado, California, quite abundant about Gilroy, Oregon, in several of the islands in Puget Sound, and wherever the climate is suitable and food abundant. This species will flourish and increase in numbers in most climates, soon adapting itself to its surroundings. As a rule, Bob White is a resident and passes his life in or near the places in which he was hatched, but in the more northern portions of his habitat, even as far south as Virginia, there appears to be a partial migration north and south in the spring and autumn, and when shooting I have often met with coveys that seemed to be traveling, though of course it is difficult to prove the fact. But it is certain that within a district where every covey which inhabits it is known and the place it usually frequents well ascertained, occasionally in the autumn other bevies will appear upon the same ground, apparently on the tramp, and which make no stay.

This bird never goes in packs or large flocks, like the plumed quails of New Mexico, Arizona, or California, but individuals of each covey, presumably one family, remain together, and even after they have been decimated by the sportsman or by furred and feathered enemies, the survivors rarely join another bevy, but keep by themselves until the recurring spring. The mating season commences according to the latitude of the birds' habitat, from March to May, and nidification from April to June. As spring begins to temper the keen blasts of winter, and the rays of the returning sun, coming from the southern limit of its journey below the Equator, cause the buds to swell upon the trees, and Nature commences to rouse herself from her winter's sleep, the clear, sharp call of the male bird is heard, as perched upon some fence rail or other elevated place in the field, he utters the well-known sounds " Bob White, ah! Bob White," expressing the latent passion of love that begins to awaken in his brave little heart. The united family that happily has kept together throughout the trying winter has become separated, and every male member is occupied with the important duty of seeking a mate. Each little feathered breast is swelling with the fires of love, and with proud carriage and eyes flashing with the desire that permeates his whole body, the cock endeavors to secure the attention of the object of his choice, to win her admiration, to attract her by his proud bearing, to cause her to listen to his sweet, earnest tones, and to reciprocate the love he offers so ardently. Ah, but she is coy, the little buff-throated hen! only looks at her lover from beneath the shelter of some bush, and makes no reply to his ringing love song, that is uttered with increasing power and passion. He leaves his coign of vantage and runs toward her, puffs up his feathers for an instant, and then leaps upon some low stump and pours out the clear " Bob White," like a challenge to all the world to come and dispute his love. Again he draws near, but she shyly moves away, looking back at him meanwhile, as if half inviting him to follow. No persuasion is needed for such an ardent knight, and he is by her side, telling his love in sweet, low tones that cause her to listen with less reserve to her gallant cavalier, who ever presses nearer, and bows before her, until captivated by his handsome presence and melodious voice, and with an answering love springing up in her own breast at length she yields a timorous consent.

The nest, placed upon the ground, is not much of a structure, merely a cavity hollowed out in the soil under a bush or fence, in pastures, or in the cotton rows in Southern States; in fact, in any spot where the locality affords the required concealment and privacy. It is well hidden and lined with grasses or stubble and sometimes arched over at the top with an aperture at the side, or again, entirely open. The eggs, which are a brilliant white, sharply pointed at one end, vary in number from twelve to twenty, and sometimes as many as thirty-two have been found, but, in such a case, more than one hen must have laid in the nest, or it may be that, when only one brood is raised in a season, the usual number may be considerably exceeded. The eggs are packed in closely with the pointed ends downward, and so skillfully are they arranged that once removed it is practically impossible to put them back again. In about twenty-four days the young appear, incubation having been performed by both sexes, chiefly, however, by the female, as is natural, and the comical little downy balls, which the chicks resemble, run about as soon as they escape from the egg. It is not often that the female is seen while incubation is progressing, but the male is frequently heard as from some stump or fence in the vicinity he whistles his clear " Bob White." In New England this call is interpreted as " more wet " or " no more wet," according to the views of the wiseheads as to the probable future condition of the weather.

The young are faithfully cared for by both parents, and scatter immediately at the note of alarm sounded by the old birds, hiding themselves in the grass or under leaves, while the parents, by the usual artifice of lameness or inability to fly, draw the intruder away from the place, to return again when all danger has passed. The note

by which the young are called together is very low and
soft, a kind of twitter. Should the nest be disturbed
before the young are hatched, or if the eggs are handled,
it is usually deserted by the birds. The chicks are able to
fly a little almost as soon as they emerge from the egg,
and (except in the northern part of the birds' dispersion)
when they are a few weeks old the male assumes the entire charge of his little family, and the female begins to lay
again her second complement of eggs, which, as a rule,
does not average as large a number as the first. In the
north one brood is generally all that is raised. The
chicks are fed by the parents on insects, but, like all
young gallinaceous birds, they are constantly in motion
and pick at everything, trying this and that small object
with great and ceaseless industry, and they soon begin
to swallow seeds, grains of different sorts, and berries.
As they grow older they become habituated to the usual
food of the adults, which consists of grain of all kinds,
especially buckwheat, of which this bird is particularly
fond, wild pease, and the seeds of various plants, with
berries, when there are any. Quail will also eat grapes,
small acorns, and beech-nuts. The parents lead their
brood to the stubbles and pick up the grain that had
been dropped during the harvest of the previous summer, and return at night to the thickets for concealment and protection. They usually visit the fields in the
early morning and again in the afternoon, but late in
the year, if the weather is cold, they frequently pass the
entire day in the open, huddled together after feeding,
basking in the comfortable warmth of the sun's rays.

The young attain their full growth in the autumn, the
period varying according as the spring has been favorable or not for incubation, as sometimes the winter
lingers so late as to prevent the nesting season from

beginning as early as usual; but from September in the South to November in the North the broods have become indistinguishable from their parents. Of course there are exceptions to this, and the first brood may have been hatched late, or the second brood delayed for some cause. I have met young birds unable to fly any distance and covered with pin-feathers as late as the last of November and beginning of December. Quail are affectionate birds, and each little family keeps always together, no member ever leaving the main body unless under compulsion, and then is very restless and unhappy until it has regained its companions.

When flushed the birds rise in a bunch, with a resounding whir of the rapidly moving wings, very disturbing to the young sportsman, and fly usually together in a straight line, and alight all at once not far from each other, when they lie close and motionless, permitting the sportsman to flush them singly. If disturbed more than once they then become widely scattered, occasionally alighting in trees, and seek the deepest thickets and most impenetrable places they can find. After they have remained unmolested for some considerable time they begin to move, and some little brown clump or tuft will stir and disclose a bird, its bright black eye glancing in every direction, the little creature all alert to every sound and motion. It gathers confidence in the stillness of its retreat, and gently utters a low *Quoi-i-hec* and listens. No response is heard, and again the same call is uttered, perhaps a little louder, and this time a similar faint cry comes in reply. Our little friend takes a few steps in the direction of the sound and calls again, and now from various parts of the field and thicket comes the cry *Quoi-i-hee, quoi-i-hee*, until, guided by their voices, the little band is again united, and their plaintive notes are heard no more, as they wander away to safer feeding grounds or place of concealment and repose.

Where the birds are much hunted they become " edu-cated," and whenever flushed fly at once to the densest thicket in the vicinity, impenetrable perhaps to both man and dog, and are safe. With such coveys one shot, as they rise before the dog, is all that can be expected. They exhibit their cunning in various ways. Some bevies, if feeding well out in the field, will begin to run toward cover as soon as a man or dog climbs over the fence, and frequently reach a place of safety before the dog has caught the scent and apprised his owner of their presence. Or, they will feed near to the fence, rarely going far from it, and slip into cover at the first alarm. Little can be done with Quail so well " edu-cated " as these.

There is no member of the gallinaceous birds more " game " than the brave little " Bob White," and none affords more diversion to the sportsman. The autumn morning breaks clear and still, and the air is crisp with the frosty breath of advancing winter as the sportsman, accompanied by his well-trained dogs, starts out for a battle with the Quail, to be waged with skill and cunning on both sides, but with unequal results, for against the pleasures of the chase, an ardent love of which is inherent in man, we must place wounds and death for the gallant birds. The dogs know as well as their master what is to be the business of the day, and as they express their delight with many a gambol and queer contortion, are observant of every field, and fre-quently toss up their heads and sniff the pure air as though the well-known scent of wandering birds was borne to their quivering nostrils. Soon the desired place is reached and, with a wave of the hand, the dogs are bidden to go forward. With a bound the fence is cleared and, regularly as the working of some faultless machine, the noble animals beat the fields on a gallop, with heads carried high and nostrils open, crossing each other's tracks at regular intervals. Suddenly one checks himself and swings around halfway, and his pace is reduced to a walk, and with careful steps and head carried on a line with his body he draws slowly forward, uncertain as yet where the birds, whose strong scent has discovered to him their presence, are located. Carefully the dog moves on, and his tail, which had been beating his sides with rapid strokes, is straightened and becomes rigid. His companion, who had overrun the scent, not being so near, sees the careful movement, and, knowing the cause, turns, and with equal care follows the direction of his mate. The first dog has now reached the vicinity of the bevy, and what a picture he presents to his master's gaze! With crouching body and tail rigid, one foreleg half raised and the paw turned backward, eyes set in a stony gaze, a frowning brow, and jaws half open, with the saliva dropping from his tongue as the hot scent wells up into his sensitive nostrils, he seems as if carved in stone, while behind him, afraid to move another step, in a similar attitude, stands motionless his mate. The sportsman moves forward and speaks in low tones words of encouragement to his four-footed friends, but the dogs stir not, and soon their master is close to the leader, when from beneath his very nose, with a whir like muffled drums, hurtling and jostling each other in their headstrong flight, rises the bevy of full-grown birds. At the sound of wings the dogs drop to the ground with their heads on the outstretched paws, and the reports of the gun ring out, stopping short some swift-flying birds that fall inert and lifeless to the earth, while the unwounded ones seek the nearest places of safety. Fresh cartridges inserted, at the snap of the barrels returning to their place the dogs spring up, and, taking the dead birds carefully in their mouths, bring them and place them in the hands of their master. What lover of the sports of the field but has witnessed some such scene as I have so vainly tried to describe—a scene stamped upon the memory to be recalled again and again in the days when failing strength and numbered years have necessitated that the old gun, the treasured companion of many a happy day, be laid aside forever, and the sports of the field be enjoyed only in the recollections of the past!

In many localities where Quail were formerly abundant they have become very scarce or quite extinct. Various causes have brought about this undesirable state of things, among which are the depredations committed by their natural enemies of the air and forest; but man is the chief culprit, and by shooting the birds in and out of season, murdering the half-grown young hardly able to fly before him, and by catching whole bevies in snares and traps of all descriptions, he has been most successful in exterminating the race from many a favorable locality. Fortunately, by introducing into such a barren spot birds from other places where they are still abundant, the evil may be remedied, for Quail soon accustom themselves to new surroundings and multiply rapidly; but as the population increases in the land, districts from which new stock can be drawn will become fewer in number, and those places, where Bob White through man's rapacity and foolishness has been exterminated, will remain tenantless of the bravest game bird in the land.

As an article of food the Quail is a very delicate and

palatable morsel, but late in the winter the flesh is apt
to be dry and rather tasteless; while those birds which
are kept from year to year in enormous cold-storage
houses, and thousands of them are, have about as much
flavor as a chip of dried wood. It is a pity that *those
cemeteries*, at least for wild game, could not be broken
up and done away with.

Quail are in the habit of roosting in or near the same
spot so long as they remain in any one locality, and such
places can frequently be determined by the droppings
on the ground. When settling for the night they
arrange themselves in a circle, each bird close to his
fellow, and with all the tails inward. This method is
advantageous for the warmth derived from the close
contact of so many little bodies, and also if alarmed or
attacked during the night by any foe, each bird can
spring directly forward and take wing unimpeded by any
of his fellows. Of course the bevy becomes greatly scattered, as each one goes away in a different direction.
In such a case they remain quiet until the day begins
to break, and then the *Quoi-i-hee* will be heard resounding from every side, as the birds gradually draw
together into a once more united family. Quail are able
to stand cold very well, provided food is abundant, but
when this is scarce and the winter severe, they suffer
greatly, and many a covey is frozen to death.

When the snow begins to fall they huddle close
together, and are frequently entirely covered with a white
mantle. If no crust is formed they easily break through,
but should they remain in their warm quarters until
the sun has partly melted the snow and it becomes frozen
again, they are unable to escape from their prison and
perish miserably. Many a covey has been found in such
a situation after the snow has melted in the spring, the

birds huddled closely together in the position in which the impenetrable drift had imprisoned them.

This species is credited by some with the power of voluntarily withholding the natural scent of the body on alighting, after having been flushed. Certainly instances are numerous, when the best dogs have been brought to a place where the birds were seen to settle, and although the ground was thoroughly covered in every direction, nothing was found. And yet after a little while, if that same ground was beaten over, the dogs would come to a point at every few moments and the birds would flush, usually singly. Again it is not unusual that when a bevy is followed immediately, when the ground on which they settled was favorable, the birds have been flushed without difficulty. If the scent was voluntarily withheld it is natural to suppose that there would be no exception to the rule, and that it would never be permitted to indicate the bird's presence after it had been flushed and thoroughly alarmed. But the instances when this is not the case are very numerous, and have been experienced by every sportsman, and they would seem to prove that the bird has not the power to withhold this evidence of its presence at will. When a bevy alights after having been flushed there are no tell-tale footsteps to give notice to the keen nostrils of the dog that any quail is near. Each bird, as it alights, remains motionless in a compact mass, every feather pressing close to the body, and occupying the smallest space possible. Unless it is almost stepped upon by the dog its presence would not likely be detected, for the bird would not move unless trodden on, and naturally there would be little or no scent from its body to betray its position. But the instant a movement was made then the tell-tale effluvia would escape, and the bird's locality be discovered. When they are readily found it may be on account of one having stirred after alighting, and, when flushed by the dog, the noise of the wings caused the others to start or change their positions, and as any movement would permit the scent to escape, they would also be quickly discovered. I do not think it at all probable the birds have any power over the natural scent of their bodies, but its absence at times is probably caused in some such way as that stated above.

COLINUS VIRGINIANUS.

Geographical Distribution.—Eastern United States from Southern Ontario and Maine to the Gulf States, but not in Florida, where it is represented by an allied race. West of the Mississippi to South Dakota (possibly introduced in the last named State from Florida), Missouri, and eastern Texas. Its range westward is being gradually extended with the settlement of the country. It has also been introduced into New Mexico, Colorado, Utah, Idaho, and on the Pacific into California, Oregon, and Washington. Breeds everywhere in its range.

Adult Male.—Forehead and stripe over the eye, extending down the side of the neck, white ; in some specimens, notably one from Massachusetts before me, this stripe and the forehead are buff, like the throat of the female. The upper side of this line is bordered with black. Top of head and neck, chestnut, with black interspersed on the former, and the feathers of the latter, with white on the webs; the chestnut being confined to an arrow-shaped mark at the tip, margined on either side with black. Sometimes this mark is all black. The amount of white seen on the neck varies greatly among individuals, and sometimes there is much buff instead of white shown. Upper part of back, light chestnut ; margin of webs of some feathers, blue-gray, vermiculated with black and more or less conspicuous. Back, rump, and upper tail-coverts varying from a grayish to a yellowish brown, blotched on middle of the back with black, and with dark brown or black triangular or arrow-headed markings along the shafts of the feathers at their tips, and irregular narrow black bars across the webs. Wings, rufous or grayish, blotched with black like the back, with buff edges on scapulars and inner secondaries forming a continuous rather broad line down either side of the back. Primaries, dark brown. Throat, white, a narrow black line under the eye. Ear-coverts, chestnut, sometimes black ; a black ring surrounds the white of the throat, commencing at ear-coverts. Breast and under parts, white or buffy white, crossed with irregular narrow black lines. Flank feathers, rich chestnut, with white edges barred with black. Some specimens have a band of chestnut across the breast beneath the black ring. Vent, white. Under tail-coverts, varying from pale to deep chestnut, with white on webs near their tips and a V-shaped black mark, but this last is sometimes absent. Tail, bluish-gray, sometimes vermiculated with black or brown near tips. Bill black. Legs and feet yellowish brown. Total length about 9½ inches; wing, 4½ ; tail, 2¾ ; tarsus, 1½ ; bill, ⅝.

There is much individual variation in the markings of Quail, although they may have a close general resemblance to each other, and birds from different sections of the United States, not inhabited by subspecies, present numerous differences both in color and style of markings. But this is only what may be expected when a species is scattered over so large a portion of the continent as is this one, and subjected to such a variety of climate as is experienced within the boundaries of its distribution. The above description will, however, answer for the average style of " Bob White " generally met with.

Adult Female.—There is not any especial difference in the plumage of the sexes, but the female can always be recognized by the buff stripe over the eye, and the buff throat. In other respects she closely resembles the male, and has about the same dimensions as are given above for him.

Downy Young.—Head, buff, with a chestnut line on forehead broadening to a patch on occiput. A black line behind the eye, and a spot of the same color at the corner of the mouth. Upper parts, chestnut ; lower parts, grayish buff, brownish on sides.

THE FLORIDA BOB WHITE.

THIS is a small, dark race of the common Bob White, and is found throughout Florida, save possibly the extreme southern portions. It was formerly very abundant, and is still in some parts of the State, but from man's persecutions and indiscriminate slaughter the birds have, in many districts, been greatly reduced in numbers. It is a very tame and confiding little creature and, like its Northern relative, prefers to live in the vicinity of man's habitations, and rarely leaves the locality in which it was hatched. It keeps to the open woods or cultivated grounds in the neighborhood of clumps of bushes or thickets of various sorts, into which it can escape from its pursuers. The nesting season in some localities begins very early, sometimes by the middle of February, but probably April is the month when incubation generally commences, and young birds have been met with early in July. Two broods are raised in a season, and the nest is placed in some retired spot hidden by a palmetto cr by thick grass and weeds.

Their habits are the same as those of the Northern bird, and they lie well before the dog, and have all the game qualities of our familiar Bob White. The average number of eggs is not so large as that found in the nests of their relative, and from ten to fourteen may be considered the extremes, though sometimes many more than the maximum given are obtained. They resemble in every respect those of Bob White.

On account of the number of broods each pair will

2. Florida Bob White.

raise in a season, and their considerable size, there is no reason why this bird should not be abundant in all the districts in which it is found, affording food and sport for multitudes of people. But so long as each person is permitted to do with them as seemeth good in his own eyes, the time cannot be far distant when it will become scarce in many parts of Florida and extinct in some. The winter brings many men to the State who hunt without ceasing, and this little bird is one of the chief objects they seek. The same covey is followed day after day until only two or three, or perhaps no birds at all are left, and then new localities are sought and fresh coveys decimated or destroyed. The negroes also snare multitudes of Quail, and on every occasion that offers take potshots at a bevy huddled together on the ground. It cannot therefore be surprising, that from man's legitimate and illegitimate killing, in connection with that accomplished by furred, feathered, and scaly foes, the lives of the Florida Quail are constantly sacrificed, and the existence of the race threatened. The food of this bird consists of seeds and berries, and its notes are the same as those of Bob White.

COLINUS VIRGINIANUS FLORIDANUS.

Geographical Distribution.—State of Florida.

Adult Male.—In its general markings this bird resembles its relative " Bob White " of the Northern United States, but is very much darker in all its coloration. The top of the head is almost black, and the white under parts are barred irregularly with jet black, and the chestnut flank feathers are marked on their outer webs with white and jet black. Lower abdomen and vent, dusky white barred with black. The back, wings, and tail are similar to those of the typical style, but much darker in all the colors, except perhaps the tail feathers, which are not much different in hue from those of the Northern " Bob White." Throat and line

over eye, pure white.   Total length about 7¾ inches ; wing, 4⅜ ;
tail, 2¾ ; tarsus, 1¼ ; bill, ½.

It will be seen from the above that the Florida bird is both
darker and rather smaller than *C. virginianus.*

Adult Female.—In her coloring this sex of the Florida Quail
bears the same relation to the male as the hen of the Northern
" Bob White " does to him, and is arrayed in hues of various
shades, as much darker as those of the male Florida bird are
darker than those of the Virginian species.   She has the buff
throat and stripe over the eye, and her dimensions are about the
same as those of the male.

Edwin Sheppard.

3. Texan Bob White.

TEXAN BOB WHITE.

E XCEPTING the Staked-Plains in the northwest part of the State, this bird is a resident of the greater portion of Texas, and grades in the east into the true Bob White of the Atlantic States. It has a general resemblance to the Northern bird, but is lighter in color, and the male has usually a pale cinnamon chestband beneath the black collar. In habits it does not differ from Bob White, and the notes and calls it utters are the same as those of the common Quail. In most parts of the State they are tame and unsuspicious, hardly taking the trouble to get out of the way of approaching danger. The males are pugnacious, though, and frequent battles occur between rivals for the affection of some shy female, who all the time regards the combatants with seeming indifference, as if not caring especially which one came off victorious.

The Texan Bob White is a bird of the lowlands, not going above 2000 feet, and is very common in the Rio Grande Valley, where it visits the ranches and feeds about the buildings. On the open prairies, where it is very numerous, it feeds on the seeds of the various grasses, grain, berries, and different species of insects from grasshoppers to ants, and, if alarmed, seeks to hide in mesquito bushes and dense thickets. Two, sometimes three broods are raised in the season. The nest, a slight cavity made in some thick grass and lined with straws and arched over with the same, contains usually from twelve to fifteen eggs, in shape and color no way

different from those of the common Bob White. Occasionally very much larger numbers are found in one nest,
but this is probably the production of more than one
hen. Eggs have been found in May, and again as late
as September, which would show that the entire summer
has been passed in hatching and tending the young.
Being so prolific, the wonder is not so much that the
birds are plentiful but rather that they are not more
numerous. This Quail, when flushed, rises with the usual
loud, whirring sound and flies in a straight line, and will
lie close and well to the dog. When undisturbed, like
the northern Bob White, it takes flight quite noiselessly,
without any of the whirring made when suddenly
startled.

The Texan Bob White has many enemies, but probably none so formidable as the rattlesnake, numbers of
which are found in the country it inhabits. Whether
the serpent crawls slyly up to the bevy when feeding or
resting, or lies in ambush and strikes the luckless birds
when passing, I know not, having never caught one
in the act of making a meal of Quail, but whatever the
method be, it is a fact that these reptiles kill many; five
having been found at one time inside of a dead rattler.
Other enemies among the wild creatures also make them
their prey, and so their number is kept from becoming
too great.

COLINUS VIRGINIANUS TEXANUS.

Geographical Distribution.—Distributed throughout western
and southern Texas. In Mexico from Guadalajara in the west, to
Tamaulipas and Nuevo Leon in the south.

Adult Male.—With the general style of markings seen in the
Northern "Bob White" this bird is lighter in coloration, and has
a tinge of olive-gray prevailing over the upper surface, which is

not, as a general thing, blotched with black to any such extent.
The lines formed by outer edges of scapulars, tertials, and inner
secondaries are very pale buff, almost white, and the bars on the
feathers are in many cases of the same color. On the upper part
of breast, beneath the black that surrounds the white throat, is a
narrow pale cinnamon band, and the white of the rest of the
under parts is irregularly barred with jet black.   Rest of plumage
like the Northern bird but paler.   Total length about 9 inches ;
wing, 4½ ; tail, 2½ ; tarsus, 1¼ ; bill, ½.

Adult Female.—General plumage marked like the male but
very pale in its general hues, in some specimens the lower back
and rump being a light olive-brown barred with buff. A band of
very pale cinnamon crosses upper part of breast, and the white
under parts are barred with dark brown.   Line over eyes, pale
buff, and the throat also pale buff, becoming almost white in the
center.   Dimensions about the same as those of the male.

As in the other forms of " Bob White," there is considerable
variation among individuals of the Texan Quail, and a description
of one bird would not be equally accurate for all, but this form
can generally be distinguished by its pale colors and narrow
cinnamon breast band.

Young.—Top of head, rufous, with a black spot in the center,
and a narrow black line from behind the eye. Upper part and
wings, rufous, mottled with blackish brown feathers, streaked and
tipped with white.   Secondaries, pale brown, mottled with blackish brown on outer webs, and barred with buffy white and tipped
with same.   Throat white.   Breast, pale brown, streaked along
the shafts of the feathers with white and vermiculated on breast
with dark brown ; rest of under parts, whitish brown, faintly
barred in the flanks with darker brown.   Bill, light horn color.

MASKED BOB WHITE.

THIS singularly colored Quail is unlike any other species inhabiting America north of Mexico. It is found in southern Arizona, Sonora, and Mexico, especially in the district lying between the gulf coast of Sonora and the Barboquivari range, and is abundant between the last-named mountains and the Plomoso. Mr. Herbert Brown of Tucson, Arizona, was the first to obtain this bird within the limits of the United States, and he says that it is found on the Sonoita Creek, about sixty miles north of the Sonora line, and from the Sonoita Valley it ranges in a westerly direction within Arizona Territory for a hundred miles through a strip of country not thirty miles wide. In a wild state this Quail does not appear to be nearly so abundant in the country it inhabits (at least on our side of the line), as are the other species of quail that are indigenous to our soil and inhabitants of the same States. The Masked Quail found in Arizona are apparently but an overflow across our border from the main body of birds in Sonora. They are met with in the valley, on the table-lands, and even as high as 6000 feet, two having been killed at that elevation in the Huachuca Mountains, in a cañon about fifteen miles north of the border; but nowhere can they be considered abundant.

Although so totally different in appearance from our common Bob White, the Masked Quail has a call note which resembles exactly that of the Northern species and, while uttering this, it perches on rocks, bushes, or other

4. Masked Bob White.

slight elevations.   It has a second note, resembling *Hoo-we*, which like the *Quoi-i-hee* of Bob White, is uttered when the birds are scattered and desirous of again coming together.   The habits of the two species are very similar, and the present one feeds on insects of various kinds, many sorts of seeds, and sometimes small leaves.   It is a very handsome bird, and in the sun the breast of the male appears red and makes him a very conspicuous object.   The body is very plump and of about the same size as Gambel's Quail.   The eggs are exactly like Bob White's in size, color, and shape, and the nest is also a similar structure, a depression in the ground hidden amid the grass, or in some retired equally well-screened position, withdrawn from the prying eyes of its enemies.

From having been taken at as lofty an elevation as 6000 feet, it would seem that this handsome species was hardy and able to withstand quite severe weather, and it might be a profitable bird to introduce in the Northern States in those localities where the original stock from various causes had disappeared.   Until, however, they had become thoroughly acclimatized, the birds would require considerable attention and care, especially in severe winters and times of heavy snows.

COLINUS RIDGWAYI.

Geographical Distribution.—Southern Arizona to Sonora, Mexico.

Adult Male.—Head, black, mixed with chestnut on top, passing into nearly all chestnut on occiput and hind-neck, the latter with occasional spots of white.   Upper part of back, chestnut, sparsely mottled with black, but rest of upper parts and wings closely barred with black and buff ; central tail feathers like the back, remainder bluish gray slightly mottled with buff near the tips.

White line over the eye ; sides of face and throat, jet black ;
entire rest of under parts, uniform cinnamon rufous ; bill, black ;
legs and feet pale brown.   Total length, 8½ inches ; wing, 4½
inches ; tail, 2¾ ; tarsus, 1⅓ ; bill, ½.

Adult Female.—The female resembles very closely that of the
Texan Quail, but is much paler, especially on the upper parts,
which have a good deal of light buff markings in bars and mottling.   The wings are particularly noticeable for their pale coloring.   The under parts are very much alike in the two birds, but the
present species has a narrower and paler cinnamon band on the
breast, and the bars on abdomen and upper breast are darker,
consequently more conspicuous.   The buff throat is very pale in
the center and toward the chin.   In dimensions the sexes are
about the same.

5. Mountain Partridge.

MOUNTAIN PARTRIDGE.

ALONG the western slopes of the Coast Range in California and Oregon, the line of its habitat inclining more to the eastward as it goes north, this beautiful bird has a rather restricted dispersion, even in the States which are its home. It has been introduced into the State of Washington, and appears to have secured a permanent foothold north of Seattle. A few crossed to the north of the Columbia, but on the south bank of that river the species has worked its way down as far as Astoria.

This Quail is rather abundant in the Willamette Valley, Oregon, and common in certain parts of California, but is very rare south of San Francisco, though it is occasionally met with in flocks of the California Partridge. It seeks moist districts and places where the rainfall is frequent. It is a shy bird, not easily found, and the flock runs along the ground for quite a distance before taking wing, and then scatters in every direction. The male has a kind of crowing note, and when a flock becomes separated its members call to each other in tones similar to the note of a hen turkey. This species is not very gregarious; that is to say, it goes in small companies of perhaps twelve to twenty, but is never seen in such great congregations as those in which the California Partridge is accustomed to assemble. The female calls her brood by clucking like the common hen, and the little creatures are great adepts at hiding on the least approach of danger. The food of the Mountain Partridge is like that of all its relatives, seeds and insects of various kinds, and it some-

times approaches the farmers' buildings for the grain that
may be scattered about.   Its flesh is very palatable, and
many are sold in the markets of the cities on the Pacific
Coast, where I have frequently seen them hanging in
large bunches.   Many are shot by sportsmen over dogs,
but more are taken, both alive and dead, in traps and
snares of many kinds.   The nest is the usual slight
depression in the ground, hidden in the grass or under
bushes or logs, or anything that will afford the requisite
privacy and shelter, and the eggs, in number from eight
to perhaps a dozen, are ovate in shape, grading from a
pale cream to a rich buff in color, and without spots.   In
size they average, according to Bendire, 34.5 by 26 milli-
meters.

OREORTYX PICTUS.

Geographical Distribution.—From the Bay of San Francisco,
California, through Oregon and Washington.   Introduced on
Vancouver Island.

Adult Male.—Top of head, sides of neck and breast, plumbeous ; entire upper parts, upper tail-coverts, and wings, deep
olive-brown, in some specimens with a rufous tinge, especially
upon the wings ; crest of lengthened straight feathers, black ;
chin, white ; entire throat, rich chestnut, bordered on the sides
with black, and separated from the olive ear-coverts and bluish
neck by a conspicuous white line ; a white spot behind the eye ;
flanks, deep chestnut, broadly barred with black and white, the
latter widest and most conspicuous ; middle of belly, white ;
under tail-coverts black, the feathers with a central line of deep
chestnut ; tail, olive-brown, mottled with black ; inner edges
of tertials broadly marked with ochraceous, forming a line on each
side of the rump ; bill, black.   Total length about 10 inches,
wing, $5\frac{8}{8}$; tail, $3\frac{1}{2}$; tarsus, $1\frac{8}{8}$; bill on culmen, $\frac{4}{8}$.

There seems to be considerable variation in the color of the
inner edges of the tertials, some birds having them white tinged
with deep buff or ochraceous, and this is confined mainly toward
the tips of the feathers ; while in others the white portion is more

or less suffused with ochraceous, and I am inclined to think it is
rather unusual to find examples with these lines entirely buff or
ochraceous. My examination of specimens seems to show that
there is always more or less white visible, and that the buff rarely
is the dominant color.

Adult Female.—Birds of this sex have little to distinguish
them from the males, but the crest is shorter ; in color of plumage
there is hardly any noticeable difference.

PLUMED PARTRIDGE.

UNLIKE its relative the Mountain Partridge, which it closely resembles, this species only approaches the seacoast in the southern parts of its range, but is essentially a bird of the drier regions of the interior, and a dweller of the mountains; and the name of "Mountain Partridge" would be much more applicable to it than it is to the one living to the westward of its habitat. It is found on both sides of the Sierra Nevada in eastern Oregon, and southward to northern Lower California. It ascends high upon the mountains, having been met with at an altitude of 7000 feet in the Sierra Nevada, and Bendire found it on Mount Kearsage in Inyo County, California, at an elevation of 10,000 feet. The most easterly point of its range is the Argus Mountains in southeastern California, where Dr. Fisher met with it. In winter it descends toward the valleys and passes this inclement season in a milder climate, but on the return of spring travels upward again, often not stopping until the snow line is reached. It is shy like the Mountain Partridge, so called, and like it goes in small coveys, and escapes by running, if possible, rather than trusting to its wings. This is the inveterate habit of all the plumed and crested Partridges, lessening very much the sport of hunting them, very trying to the human, and perfectly exasperating and bewildering to the dog. In spring the male utters a loud clear call, something like *Pheu-i-é*, *Pheu-i-é*, while mounted upon some stump or rock, and the mating season commences about April.

Edwin Sheppard.

6. Plumed Partridge.

The nest, a slightly contrived affair, is placed in some well-concealed spot on the ground, and the bird lays about the same number of eggs as the Mountain Partridge. These are smooth and glossy, varying from a pale cream to a reddish-buff in color, and are without any spots. In size they average about the same as those of the last species.

The Plumed Partridge is a beautiful bird, one of the largest members of the Tribe, and with its long upright slender plumes decorating the head, and its strong contrasting hues, presents a very handsome and gallant appearance. Although resembling very closely in coloration the Mountain Partridge, it can be distinguished by its hind-neck, which has the same plumbeous color as the breast, while its relative has this part olive-brown or umber. By some, however, the two forms are not considered even as subspecifically distinct, but as their habitats can be fairly well defined, it would seem best to recognize the two races. When alarmed this bird utters a sharp quick note like " quit " several times repeated; and evinces the same anxiety and solicitude for its young as do other members of the Family by feigning lameness and inability to fly, uttering all the time a shrill, plaintive cry. While the old bird is thus endeavoring to draw the intruder away, the young are busily taking care of themselves, scattering in all directions and hiding under leaves or in bushes, where they squat and remain motionless, effectually concealed by their close resemblance in color to the surrounding objects. Their food consists of insects, seeds, buds, and leaves of various plants, and grain if obtainable.

OREORTYX PICTUS PLUMIFERUS.

Geographical Distribution.—Both sides of the Sierra Nevada, and in eastern Oregon and to the Panamint Mountains and Mount Magruder, Nevada. In California from San Francisco Bay to the Argus Mountains.

Adult Male.—Forehead and chin, white ; head, hind-neck, upper part of back and breast, plumbeous ; long black crest from occiput ; throat, deep chestnut, bordered on sides with black, outside of which is a line of white ; wings, back, and upper tail-coverts, grayish olive ; flanks, deep chestnut, barred broadly with white, beneath which is a narrow black bar ; abdomen, chestnut ; under tail-coverts black, the feathers having a central line of deep chestnut ; inner edges of tertials, narrowly lined with white, forming two lines on back ; dimensions about the same as those of the *O. pictus.*

There is no particular difference in the coloring of the sexes, and the female is recognizable chiefly by her shorter crest.

7. San Pedro Partridge.

SAN PEDRO PARTRIDGE.

I HAVE never seen this bird alive. Its range appears to be restricted to the San Pedro Mountains, Lower California, where it is found from the foothills to the tops of the loftiest peaks, estimated to be over 12,000 feet in height. The discoverer of this race, Mr. Anthony, writes to Captain Bendire that it is not common below 2500 feet of elevation, that the call notes are a soft, far-reaching "Chay chay," like the notes of a flute in sweetness. The alarm note was a soft "ch-ch-ch-e-e-ea, ch-e-e-ea," which increased with the appearance of danger to a harder "kee-ke-ea," and this last cry is taken up by every member of the covey as they draw away. When taking wing a loud "pit pit" is often heard. In his remarks on this race, Mr. Anthony says he found this bird quite abundant from 6000 to 10,000 feet above the sea, occurring wherever water and timber afforded it drink and shelter ("seeking the shelter of the manzanitas, from whence their clear, mellow notes were heard morning and evening, so suggestive of cool brooks and rustling pines, but so out of place in the hot, barren hills of that region").

Flocks wintered around this camp at Valladores, six miles from the base of the range at an elevation of 2500 feet, and a few pair bred there, but by March nearly all had disappeared, moving higher up the mountains. The nest was a mere hollow under a manzanita bush, and filled with dry leaves of the lilac and manzanita, and the eggs are creamy white and unspotted.

OREORTYX PICTUS CONFINIS.

Geographical Distribution.—" Mountains of San Pedro range, Lower California, reaching to valleys in winter."—*Anthony.*

Adult Male.—" Back wings and tail, ashy brown with slight olive wash ; inner secondaries and tertials bordered with white, forming, when wings are closed, two parallel bars of white; foreparts above and below, slaty blue, slightly grayer above; belly, rich chestnut, banded on the sides with bars of white and black ; flanks, rufous ; tibia, ashy ; crissum, velvety black, streaked with chestnut ; throat, chestnut, bordered laterally with a narrow black line, which in turn is bordered with white ; a white mask surrounding the bill and changing to grayish on forehead.   Arrow plumes black."—*Anthony.*

Edwin Sheppard.

8. Scaled Partridge.

SCALED PARTRIDGE.

SCALED Partridge, Blue, White Top-Knot, and White Crested Quail, by all of which names this species is known, is found from western Texas, through New Mexico to southern Arizona in the United States, and also south into northern Mexico. North and east of the White and Mogallon mountains it does not seem to go, while Fanin County, Texas, and the Colorado River in Arizona, are the eastern and western limits of its dispersion within our boundaries. My experience with this beautiful bird has been gained in New Mexico, in the southern portions, on the mesas lying near the Mogallon Mountains, and westward into Arizona. It does not frequent timber, but dwells in the open, on the high plateaus, where the cactus grows, and for this reason it is sometimes known as the Cactus Quail. It seems to be independent of water, and frequents dry and sandy districts, where vegetation is exceedingly sparse, indeed almost absent, and where there is nothing to shelter it either from the heat or its enemies, save a few clumps of cacti, yuccas, and similar stunted plants, scattered over the plain; and the more spiny and thorny the bushes the more the Blue Quail loves to frequent them.

This species goes in flocks sometimes of considerable size, several broods probably joining together, and I have always found them exceedingly shy and wary, commencing to run as soon as my presence was discovered. They usually went in Indian file, following some one bird that

appeared to act as a leader, though occasionally in their
haste the main body would overtake him, and then for
a space they would continue on bunched up all together,
gradually straggling out again into a long line. The
body was held very erect and stiff while running, the tail
almost touching the ground, and the white crest was
spread out in a fan shape, showing very conspicuously.
This bird runs with great speed, and seems to be able to
keep it up for a long distance, and flies with much reluctance, alighting almost immediately and beginning to run
at once. When compelled to take wing, it rises with the
usual *whir-r-r*, and proceeds on a slightly curved line,
rarely straight ahead, and if, on alighting, it should stop
for a moment, it is always under the cover of some cactus
or other low bush, which affords a place of concealment,
and from which it can watch its pursuer, before starting
to run again.

A dog is practically useless for hunting the Scaled
Partridge, for if he is well broken and attempts to point a
covey, the birds will run several hundred yards while he
is standing, and then will add several hundred more,
while he is trailing them, and the poor animal becomes
bewildered and disgusted and is apt to run also. I know
nothing so trying to the patience of a sportsman as the
tactics of this species, unless it be the similar habits of
other Crested Quail. As a rule this species was not very
much hunted in the localities I met with it, and it always
seemed to me rather singular that they should be so
wary, for that is an attribute that wild creatures usually
acquire after having made the acquaintance of man and
learned that his presence always brought wounds and
death, and that safety to themselves was only to be obtained by leaving his vicinity as soon as possible. But
these birds seem instinctively to have ascertained this

fact before they ever saw a human being, and decamp at once whenever a man appears.

This Partridge is a dweller of high table-lands and is found at an altitude of 6000 to 7000 feet, and subsists mainly upon various kinds of small seeds, grain if any is grown in the vicinity, berries, buds or tender parts of plants, and insects of different kinds. When alarmed it utters a curious low *boom*-like sound, at other times a short, quick note, difficult to indicate by letters. There is no difference in the plumage of the sexes, the female being as gayly clad as the male, and in this respect the species constitutes an exception among the other varieties of Partridge inhabiting the United States, for in all of these, the females are rather differently arrayed from the males, with conspicuous markings indicating their sex. The nesting season begins about May, and generally two broods are raised, and sometimes even three. The slightly formed nest is placed on the ground under some sheltering bush, or in a corn, or other grain field, in alfalfa grass, and sometimes in potato fields. The eggs, in number usually about a dozen, vary from creamy white to pale buff in color, and are covered with various-sized reddish brown or fawn-colored spots, regularly distributed over the shell. Sometimes these spots are so small that they are barely distinguishable. The shape is subpyriform. This species seems to prefer to make its nest on the upper mesas, even among the foothills of the mountain ranges, returning in winter, if the weather is severe, to the lower lands and river bottoms. I have never met the coveys in thickets, or amid underbrush, or in timber even if very open, but it is evidently a bird of the treeless country and cacti-covered plains. Doubtless, like many another species, its habits vary in different localities, and it suits itself to its surroundings. If by chance Gambel's

Partridge should inhabit the same district as the Scaled Partridge, the two species associate together apparently on most amicable terms, but the kind of ground each prefers is usually of so different a character that they are not often found together. The Blue Partridge is a handsome bird and attractive in spite of its unsportsmanlike habits, the markings of its plumage causing it to appear as if covered with imbricated scales, a rather unique dress among its brethren.

CALLIPEPLA SQUAMATA.

Geographical Distribution.—Western Texas, New Mexico, and Southern Arizona. Valley of Mexico.

Adult.—Head, brown or brownish gray, varying in depth of hue among individuals ; tip of crest, white ; throat, pale buff. Hind-neck, upper parts of back and breast, bluish gray, each feather bordered with black, giving the plumage a scaly appearance ; scapulars, wings, lower back, and rump, pale brown; upper tail-coverts and tail, bluish gray; flanks, bluish gray, streaked with white; rest of lower parts, pale buff; feathers, margined with blackish brown; bill, black. Total length, 9¼ inches; wing, 5 ; tail, 4¼ ; tarsus, 1⅜. There is no difference whatever in the coloring of the plumage in the sexes, and males and females are indistinguishable except by dissection.

9. Chestnut-Bellied Scaled Partridge.

CHESTNUT-BELLIED SCALED PARTRIDGE.

THIS subspecies, at times indifferently distinguishable from the Scaled Partridge, has a very restricted range, being found within our limits only in the lower Rio Grande Valley, in Texas, and across the border in eastern Mexico. Among the foothills of the Rio Grande, about one hundred miles from the coast, as stated by my friend Mr. Geo. B. Sennett, is the eastern limit of this bird. In its habits, selection of food, and character of the country it dwells in, it closely resembles the Scaled Partridge. Some specimens are strongly and broadly marked with chestnut on the belly, this at times being very dark in color; but this varies greatly, both in hue and in the space it covers, until some individuals are met with that are very difficult to assign to either the species or the race. They grade in a large series of examples, directly from one to the other, so as to make it impossible to say where one form begins and the other ends. This bird raises two broods in a season and commences to lay as early as March, depositing from twelve to twenty eggs in a slight cavity in the ground scraped out under some thick bushes or clump of grass, and lined with grass. The eggs vary from a pale creamy white to a rich buff, covered all over with reddish brown spots, from the size of a pin's head to a considerable blotch. There is great variation in both color and markings, and it is very difficult, if not impossible, at times to distinguish those belonging to the two forms apart.

CALLIPEPLA SQUAMATA CASTANEIGASTRA.

Geographical Distribution.—Lower Rio Grande Valley, Texas, Northeastern Mexico.

Adult.—Head, brownish gray, darker than that of *C. squamata*, and the throat is also a darker buff; the blue of the breast and back is more of a decided tint, as is also the brown of the wings and lower back; lower parts, dark buff, ochraceous in some specimens, with a more or less extensive patch of rusty chestnut on the belly; upper tail-coverts and tail, bluish gray; there is more white on the crest, in certain examples, the feathers being nearly all white; in general appearance this is a darker bird than the typical style, but the chestnut patch varies greatly in extent among individuals, being reduced at times to barely a trace, and the two styles grade into each other by imperceptible degrees, until it is impossible to designate where one ends and the other begins; in size the two forms are about equal, and there is no difference in the color of plumage or style of markings between the sexes.

10. California Partridge.

CALIFORNIA PARTRIDGE.

THIS is the species found in the coast region of California, northward to Vancouver's Island, as separated from its paler relative of the interior of Oregon, southward to Cape St. Lucas.

It is a very handsome bird, perhaps not quite equal in this respect to its beautiful cousin Gambel's Partridge, with which the uninitiated frequently confound it, but with this solitary exception no other species can dispute successfully its claim to be the handsomest member of the family.

It was not indigenous to the State of Washington, its range not extending farther north than Oregon, but it was introduced both there and in the islands of Puget Sound, and also in Vancouver Island (where I met with it), and has increased greatly in all these places. It is a resident species, does not migrate, frequents cañons and bushy hillsides, also fields, is often seen in enormous flocks, as if many broods had united together, and runs rapidly over the ground, preferring to escape if possible by this method than to make use of its wings. These great flocks or packs are only formed in the fall of the year after the breeding season is over, and occasionally the number of birds gathered together will amount to several hundred, and they are then wilder than at other times. In the spring these packs gradually break up, and the birds commence to mate in March, if the winter has not lingered longer than usual.

This species, like many others that have been persistently hunted and trapped, has greatly decreased in number in many localities where it was formerly very abundant, and the large packs mentioned above are not very often seen at the present time, except in districts far removed from towns or villages, in which every man carries a gun. The average number of eggs in the nest is about fifteen, and they have a creamy white, or buff ground color, minutely dotted or blotched with chestnut-brown, olive-gray, or pale rufous. The nest is almost always placed on the ground, sometimes without any attempt at concealment, but usually under some log or bush, or close to a stump. Instances are known, however, where this species has nested in trees at no great height from the ground. Incubation is carried on for about three weeks, and the young run as soon as hatched.

The California Partridge is naturally of a tame and confiding disposition, and, when not molested, will approach farm buildings and remain near the dwellings feeding among the poultry, but, when much hunted, soon becomes wild and wary, shunning man and all his belongings. The food consists of seeds, berries, and tender plants, and various insects, and it is upon these last that the chicks are usually fed. The male does not assist the females in incubating the eggs, but mounts guard close at hand, and utters his call note at intervals. The old birds tend the young carefully, and are very watchful of any danger threatening their chicks, which at the first note of warning scatter in all directions and hide under anything that will afford a cover, from a dried leaf to a log or bush, and if nothing of the kind is at hand, will squat upon the ground, remaining motionless until the cause of their fear has departed.

LOPHORTYX CALIFORNICUS.

Geographical Distribution.—California coast region, as far south as Monterey. Introduced into Oregon, Washington, and British Columbia.

Adult Male.—Forehead, buff; shafts of feathers, black; occiput, dark chestnut bordered anteriorly, and on the sides with black, followed by a line of pure white; line from bill to eye, white; chin and throat, jet black, bordered all around from behind the eye with white, which is again margined narrowly with black; back of neck and upper part of back, blue, the feathers margined with black and a minute bluish white spot at tip; entire upper parts, deep smoke brown; the inner edge of tertials, deep buff or ochraceous, forming two conspicuous lines; sometimes the outer edges of the secondaries are margined with ochraceous; primaries, dark brown; breast, deep blue; belly, deep buff, the feathers margined with black; flanks, smoke brown, streaked with white; abdomen, dark chestnut, the feathers with black margins; vent and under tail-coverts, deep buff, with broad central streaks of dark brown; bill, black; crest, black, very narrow at the base, widening out and curving forward at the tip; all the feathers, of which there are about six, inclosed between the webs of the anterior plume. Total length of bird, 10 inches; wing, 4½; tail, 4; tarsus, 1¼; bill, ½.

Adult Female.—With certain resemblances to the male, the female differs in having a shorter, chestnut brown crest; head, smoky gray without white or black markings; no chestnut patch on abdomen, and the scaly markings less pronounced; otherwise she resembles the male, the colors, however, being less clear and more subdued.

VALLEY PARTRIDGE.

PALER in color than its relative of the coast, the present race inhabits the interior of Oregon, Nevada, and California as far to the southward as Cape St. Lucas, frequents the valleys and foothills of the mountains, and ascending the latter in Lower California to an elevation of about 8000 or 9000 feet. It is found on both slopes of the Sierra Nevada, and goes east to Death Valley, and along the Mojave River until it reaches the western limits of Gambel's Partridge. In the upper part of the Willamette Valley, Oregon, it is abundant, but in the lower part is supplanted by the California Partridge. It has been introduced into Utah, and flourished there in all suitable localities. It withstands cold very well, for Bendire states (Life Hist. N. Am. B. p. 27), that in the upper Klamath Valley, Oregon, he found a small covey, which passed successfully through the winter of 1882, though the thermometer registered more than once considerably below zero, and the next spring there were two coveys of half-grown birds. In Lower California very dry seasons occasionally occur, and it is a rather singular fact, and this has been proved by several careful observers, that during such periods the Valley Quail do not breed, but the large flocks that are formed during the autumn remain unbroken all summer. The cause of this curious condition of affairs may be the scarcity of seeds and tender grasses, which from lack of moisture have not appeared in the customary abundance. However, if the winter rainfall has been of the usual quantity, then the

11. Valley Partridge.

coveys break up in March, and mating begins. This fact is a very remarkable one, as it shows the suppression of the amatory instinct (we can hardly imagine at the will of the bird), at a time when, if it was allowed to have its usual sway with the consequent result, the probability would be that the young would perish from lack of food. But it would seem that the birds' volition had nothing to do with the case, for, as Mr. Anthony states (in a letter to Captain Bendire given in the work already cited), individuals obtained by him in April, May, and June, during one of these dry seasons, exhibited but a very slight development of the ovaries. The nesting season begins in March, perhaps a little later in the northern portion of its habitat, and the males at this time are very pugnacious, and frequent battles occur among them for the possession of some particular fair one. The challenge call of the male is clear and loud, and he also has a low, tender note, which seems to be uttered solely for the female, and resembles the syllables *ah-hooh*. The nest is a very primitive affair; very often the eggs are deposited on the bare ground, under some bush, log, or by the side of a rock, or in similar situations as are selected by the California Partridge, and the number, coloring, and marking of the eggs are the same as those of the species just named.

The habits and food of the two birds are very much alike, as would be supposed, and the present race runs as swiftly, exhibits the same unwillingness to lie before a dog, takes to a tree or bush quickly, and evinces the same indisposition to fly as is displayed by its relative. If the flock is met suddenly, the birds utter a cry that sounds very much as if they were trying to swear at the intruder in Spanish, and many an angry *ca-raho* is hurled at his head in earnest tones, as if the startled birds were indignantly warning the trespasser away from their premises. This race is fond of frequenting thickets, hedge-rows along the cultivated fields, and is naturally tame and of a sociable disposition. This trustful nature, however, is rapidly changed to one of suspicion and alarm after the birds have had a short experience with their great enemy man, and when that is the case his appearance is announced by a sharp note, resembling *pip-pip-pip*, and the flock is off on a quick run ending, if closely pursued, in a short flight and a general scattering all over the locality. As a game bird, to hunt with a dog, they are very unsatisfactory and disappointing, in no way to be compared to the brave little Bob White of the Eastern States.

LOPHORTYX CALIFORNICUS VALLICOLA.

Geographical Distribution.—Interior of Oregon, California, and Nevada, East to the Panamint Mountains, South to Cape St. Lucas.

Adult Male.—In general appearance this bird resembles the California Partridge; the pattern of markings and distribution of colors being almost precisely similar, but there is a consistent variation in the hues themselves; the color and markings of the heads of the two forms are alike, and the crests are the same, but the upper parts of the Valley Partridge are grayish brown, and the inner margins of tertials are white; the belly is white or buffy white, and the flanks grayish brown; it is altogether a bluer or more grayish blue bird, and much lighter beneath when contrasted with the typical styles; in size it equals the *L. californicus.*

Adult Female.—Forehead, bluish gray; occiput, rusty brown; crest, very short, snuff brown; in the color of the upper parts she resembles the male, and the margins of the tertials are buffy white ; throat, brownish white, streaked with darker brown; breast, bluish gray, flanks, same color, streaked with white; lower breast and abdomen, white, the feathers margined with black; under tail-coverts, bronzy brown, margined with pale buff or whitish; the female is conspicuous beneath by the amount of white exhibited, and like the male she is lighter in color than the corresponding sex of the typical form; there are no black or white markings on the head.

Young, Half Grown.—Forehead, bluish gray, streaked with white ; feathers margined with black, rest of head on top, dark rusty brown; short crest, rusty brown, black in center; back of neck, bluish gray, vermiculated with light brown, rest of back bluish gray, feathers margined with blackish brown; wings, rusty brown, barred and vermiculated with black; sides of head and throat, buff, streaked with bluish gray; breast pale bluish-gray; rest of under parts, buffy white, indistinctly barred with bluish gray; tail blue, barred and mottled on edge of webs with black.

GAMBEL'S PARTRIDGE.

WHILE disputing the palm for beauty of dress and gallant appearance with its relative the California Partridge, the present species possesses all of the same disagreeable traits when he is regarded in the light of a game bird. In his legs does he trust, and the rocky cañons and hillsides are his delight, and when met with at the base of these often lofty and steeply ascending cliffs, instead of flying as any well-mannered Quail would do, he runs with all his might, leaping from stone to stone, dodging behind one bowlder after another until he becomes a mere speck above one, or disappears altogether. The range of this handsome bird extends from western Texas, through New Mexico and Arizona to California, where it meets the Valley Partridge in San Bernardino County, the Colorado desert proving an effective barrier to its extension farther westward. It is also found in southeastern Utah, and was introduced at Fort Union in northern New Mexico. It also crosses our southern border and is a resident of northwestern Mexico. Any kind of a locality within its dispersion seems to be perfectly satisfactory to this bird; whether it be a dry and sandy stretch blistering in torrid heat, or a place rocky and bare of leafy covering, or tracts hidden by the densest and most impregnable thickets—they are all the same to Gambel's Quail. From my experience, however, in hunting them, I should say, if they had any choice of locality it lay between dense clumps, matted with vines and bristling with thorns, into and through

which nothing living could penetrate save themselves, or mountain sides that ascend in a direct line and which are covered with jagged stones and slippery bowlders, over which the light-footed birds pass without effort, stopping occasionally to look down and jeer at the struggling, panting mortal below who is striving to conquer the ascent, and when the pursuer had arrived at the summit, the Quail, it would be discovered, had run to the edge of another cañon, into which they flew at the first appearance of the sportsman, and began the ascent from below on the opposite side, leaving the hunter gazing at them across the great gulf that rolled between. If there is another species of game bird more tantalizing and vexatious in its manners, and more utterly lost to all the finer feelings that should compel it to conform to the recognized rules that govern field sports, I happily do not know of it, and have no wish to meet with it, if existing.

This species is dependent upon water, never going far away from brook or spring, and its presence is a pretty sure indication that a supply of the necessary fluid is near at hand. Gambel's Quail is generally very abundant in the localities it frequents, and the coveys of trim, gay-looking birds are seen daily running about chasing insects, dusting themselves in the roads or sandy spots, and uttering all the while a soft low *quot* or *woot*. When alarmed, they commence to run, following some leader in outstretched line, or else in bunches when each looks out for himself, dodging behind every bush and stone, and generally striving to reach some dense thicket, or some rocky hillside up which they climb with surprising rapidity. It is, at first, almost impossible to make them take wing, and they will only fly when compelled to do so by their pursuer appearing right among them,

and then they proceed but a short distance before alighting, and commence to run again. If the ground per-
mits the covey to be followed rapidly and continuously,
and the birds find that running is of no avail, they can
then be flushed, and they fly swiftly, generally on a level
about six or eight feet above the ground, but in a curving
direction, not straight forward for any distance, and if
the covey becomes well scattered the birds will sometimes lie well and flush singly; but this is exceptional,
and a state of affairs only arrived at by a long, persistent,
and fatiguing pursuit. I imagine that most of the birds
that are obtained by the gun are shot upon the ground.
Very unsportmanlike, but after one learns their tricks
and their manners the natural feeling of denunciation
against such a practice that is possessed by all lovers of
dog and gun, somehow does not seem to be so easily
aroused in those who have followed these birds for food
or recreation. If, however, the sportsman fails to obtain
either of these, there is one thing he does get without
stint—exercise.

Gambel's Partridge bears well great extremes of tem-
perature and is apparently quite as comfortable where
the thermometer indicates 100° in the shade, as in
the keen, rarefied air that blows around the mountain
tops at an elevation of 8000 or 9000 feet. When the
heat is as great as that mentioned above, this species
seeks the bottoms of the cañons, or the banks of the
creeks, and keeps in the shade of the dense thickets
usually found in such situations, or, as is frequently
the case, perches in the trees. This custom is habitual
to it, for it is quite an arboreal bird, taking refuge
on the branches of trees or bushes if suddenly
alarmed, or when the members of a flock become scattered after having been compelled to take wing. The

mating season commences quite early in the spring, say the month of April, and the male presents a very handsome appearance as with erect body, dignified movements, puffed-out feathers and trailing, trembling wings, he moves sedately before the gaze of his shy lady-love. She is a modestly attired little body, similar, but still quite different in dress to her lord, lacking the strongly contrasting colors upon the head, and the great black patch on the belly. The glossy, jet black, graceful plume of many feathers that decorates the head of the male, opening and closing, as his frequent changes of feelings exert their influence, is in the female reduced to small proportions, and dusky in hue.

The nest is simply a hollow scratched out in the soil, sometimes lined with grass or leaves, and concealed from view by tall grass, or by some overhanging bush, or else hidden away amid the vegetation that springs up in the dry beds of the creeks. In fact any spot that will afford the necessary protection and concealment is taken advantage of, and the eggs removed from the view of prying enemies. Doubtless, however, many are taken by reptiles such as snakes of various kinds, and even the Gila Monster has been known to have made a meal on the eggs of this species. The usual number found in a nest is from twelve to fifteen; and these have a ground color varying from a creamy white to a pale buff, irregularly spotted and blotched with dark seal, sometimes almost blackish, brown, drab, or rufous, all suffused with a peculiar purplish bloom. Occasionally a nest is found placed in a tree, or cactus, a few feet from the ground, the bird, doubtless, having lost the eggs previously laid, had sought a more secure refuge from her terrestrial foes. The period of incubation extends to about four weeks, and probably two broods are raised in a season. The birds do not seem to have any regular time to commence laying, some being much later than others, and on this account, and the number of broods raised, young or half-grown birds are met with nearly throughout the entire summer. The pretty little downy chicks run as soon as hatched, and soon become exceedingly expert in hiding, which they are quick to do at the warning chirp of the mother, squatting close to the ground and remaining absolutely motionless, or crawling under leaves, or any shelter that is available. Danger past, at a cluck from the anxious mother, who all the time has probably been crouching near by, watching her brood, the chicks gather around her, and are led to a more retired and secure locality. When able to use their wings and fly with some degree of freedom, the young take refuge in the trees and perch on the branches, but as they grow older the one particular habit they have inherited prevails over all the rest, and their legs are depended upon for escape more than upon any other means at their disposal, and they run with considerable swiftness, only using the wings as the last resort.

Gambel's Partridge has many enemies, foremost among which is man, both white and red, who destroys vast numbers both with gun and snares of various ingenuity. Hawks, wolves, foxes, and other predatory animals kill numbers, and doubtless many fall a prey to rattlesnakes and other reptiles. Still if the species only had to combat with its natural enemies, it would probably be able to maintain itself in undiminished numbers, but whenever man, especially Caucasian man, takes a hand in destroying, the time of diminution and final extinction of any wild creature is near at hand.

This Partridge has a number of calls, which it utters at various times and on especial occasions, some of which

are very difficult to represent on paper. At the commencement of the pairing season it gives voice to a clear,
ringing note, usually uttered from some slight eminence,
which has been compared to the syllables *yuk-käe-ja*
by Captain Bendire and *killink* by Dr. Coues, each
syllable distinctly uttered and the last two somewhat
lengthened. These notes strike each hearer so differently that it is impossible to write them down and convey
to each the impression he has received. To me the three-
syllabled word given above more clearly describes the
note as it was heard by me, but doubtless many others
would recognize it better by the word of two syllables as
given by Dr. Coues. This note, or cry, is equivalent to
the Bob White of our Northern bird. The alarm note is
well indicated by Captain Bendire as *crä̀er, crä̀er*, frequently repeated; a rasping, harsh sound, in uttering
which many members of a covey join. At other times,
when undisturbed, a soft *pcct* is heard, followed on
the slightest alarm by a sharp *quit*, succeeded by the
pattering of little feet upon the dry leaves as the covey
hurries away. It is a gentle, beautiful little creature, and
without Gambel's Partridge, with all its unsportsmanlike
ways, many an arid and rock-strewn district would be
deprived of its chief attraction.

LOPHORTYX GAMBELI.

Geographical Distribution.—Western Texas, New Mexico, and
Arizona to San Bernardino County, California. Also in Southern
Utah and Nevada, and Northwestern Mexico.

Adult Male.—Top of head and nape, bright chestnut; forehead,
black, interspersed with grayish above the bill, and crossed by a
narrow white line between the eyes; a white stripe from behind
the eye to back of ear-coverts, bordered above with black; chin,
throat, and side of face beneath the eyes, black, bordered all

around with white; back and sides of neck, lead color, each feather narrowly bordered with brownish black; entire upper parts, grayish blue, darkest on upper tail-coverts, where the feathers are faintly margined with white; tail, pale blue; wings like the back, but with a brownish tinge; the inner webs of the tertials broadly margined with white, and the outer webs of those nearest the primaries narrowly margined with yellowish white, forming a horizontal bar when the wing is closed; primaries, brown, grayish on the outer webs; upper part of breast, pale blue; lower part to abdomen, bright buff; flanks, dark chestnut, with a conspicuous white stripe along the shaft; abdomen, black, flanked by bright buff feathers, with a white stripe in the center, bordered with chestnut; vent and under tail-coverts, pale buff with grayish brown central stripe tinged with chestnut ; an upright plume composed of five or six black feathers, curving forward, and the webs turned backward, each overlapping the one behind, rises from the forehead, sometimes bending over the bill; bill, black; feet and legs, horn color. Total length, 10 inches; wings, 4¾; tail, 4½; bill, ½; legs, 1¼.

Adult Female.—Differs from the male in having the upper parts tinged with olive-green; top of head, olive-brown; throat, dark buff, streaked with bluish gray; upper part of breast, grayish blue, rest of under parts pale buff, the feathers narrowly margined with blackish chestnut; flanks, chestnut with central white stripe ; under tail-coverts, bronzy brown, margined with pale buff; wings as in the male, the tertials less conspicuously margined with white; tail, purplish blue; a short brownish black bunch of feathers rises from top of head, but does not bend forward; bill, black; legs and feet, horn color. Total length, 9¾ inches; wing, 4¾, tail, 4½; bill, ½; legs, 1¼.

Edwin Sheppard.

13.   Massena Partridge.

MASSENA PARTRIDGE.

KNOWN in the territories it frequents within our borders as the Black, Black-bellied, and Fool Quail, the
Massena Partridge is the most fantastically colored of all
the family to which it belongs, with a head striped and
marked like that of the clown in a pantomime. It is
however, a very handsome bird, though bizarre in its
pattern of coloration, and would attract attention wherever seen. It ranges in more or less abundance from
western Texas in the vicinity of San Antonio, through
New Mexico, and into Arizona as far as Fort Whipple,
which is about its western limit. It has been observed
in the upper Rio Grande valley near Taos, and south of
our limits inhabits northwestern Mexico, ranging upon
the mountains at varying elevations of from 4000
to over 9000 feet. It seems to be more of a bird of the
hills than are most of the other species of Partridge,
and prefers the high mesas and valleys that lead up
into the lofty mountain ranges. In the United States
I do not think this Partridge can be called abundant
anywhere, and the localities in which it is found are
apparently restricted; whether or not on account of some
especial food it subsists upon I am unable to say. When
met with it is generally in small bunches, as if composed
of one family, and the birds are extremely gentle and
confiding, hardly moving out of the way of either man
or beast. At times this species seems to be entirely
insensible to fear, and when approached suddenly, either
squats down on the ground or walks a few steps to one

side, sometimes merely standing perfectly still and regarding the intruder with a glance that may mean inquiry or curiosity. It does not run like Gambel's and other plumed Partridges, but if wishing to escape, and this resolution is not often taken without considerable deliberation, a covey will rise with a whir and fly very rapidly in a direct line; usually the birds uttering a clucking note as they speed along. As a rule, they do not fly very far, but scatter and remain in the place where they alight, and can then be flushed singly. In this respect their habits are far superior from a sportsman's point of view to those of the other Partridges that dwell in the same countries. From its gentle disposition and apparent unwillingness to move, frequently when almost trodden upon, this bird has gained the sobriquet of " Fool Quail," and it has often been killed with a stick in the hands of its pursuer. It may be that it is more numerous in a locality than indications would warrant the supposition, for, on account of its habit of crouching or remaining motionless, a covey could easily escape unnoticed in the grass, although the passer-by was but a very short distance away.

The Massena Partridge is fond of dusting itself in the roads if there are any, or in sandy places, and when so occupied does not resort to cover until closely approached. In summer they ascend high upon the mountains, coming down, when snow begins to fall, to low altitudes, and occasionally the birds breed at as lofty an elevation as 7000 feet. Although I have never seen the two species actually together, yet I have known the Massena and Gambel's Partridge to occupy the same district in winter, and it is not an unusual thing in New Mexico to obtain both species in one afternoon by the same gun. The reason that the Fool Quail is so confiding is probably that the waste places it frequents are not much resorted to by man, and hence its acquaintance with its chief enemy and destroyer has been of too limited a character for it to acquire that shy and wild disposition a full knowledge of the ways and power of the human biped always brings to every creature of the woods and plains. It may be that in some places where the Massena Partridge has been much hunted that it is as wild and wary as are the other species of this group, but wherever I have seen it, the birds have always possessed the gentle disposition already mentioned. So far as I am aware it never goes in large flocks, but is met with in small companies, and not infrequently three or four birds only are seen together. It appears to be as altogether different in its ways from other Partridges as it is from them in general appearance. It is a plump little bird, and has a manner of walking with a rounded back and humped up body, and exhibits very little of the elegance of form and gracefulness of carriage so characteristic of Gambel's and the California Partridge, or even the Blue Quail. But its fantastically colored head, flanks dotted like the plumage of a guinea fowl, and short, stumpy tail give to it an appearance peculiarly its own and in no way approached by any other Partridge. The nest is a hollow scratched out of the soil, lined with grass, and hidden by the grass growing around, or else placed under a bush or some dead limb lying near the ground, surrounded by grass. The eggs are pure white, very glossy, and about ten in number.

When there are any grain fields in the vicinity of its habitat this Partridge will pick up the kernels lying about, but its chief food, at least in certain localities, seems to be small bulbous roots, and perhaps the restricted area in which these are found may in a measure account for the bird's apparently scattered dispersion in the districts it frequents. Its indolent ways would seem to offer it a prey to any active animal, and doubt-less it is easily secured by Hawks, Owls, and four-footed depredators always on the watch for a toothsome morsel. In some localities where, not long since, it was fairly abundant, as in New Mexico in the vicinity of the Gila River and around Silver City, it has now become scarce, as it proved to be such an easy victim that the coveys were soon decimated or quite exterminated, and unless its disposition becomes greatly changed and it learns how more effectually to protect itself from its enemies, it will probably soon cease to exist after its habitats have been invaded by those who shoot either for pleasure or profit.

CRYTONYX MONTEZUMA.

Geographical Distribution.—Western Texas, New Mexico, and Arizona. Table-lands of Mexico.

Adult Male.—Forehead, black; with white stripe passing upward from nostril; top of head, pale brown, barred with black; occiput, richer brown, unmarked, feathers forming a short thick crest; rest of head, white, with a plumbeous stripe from angle of mouth, extending in a curved line to beneath the ears, meet-ing a broader line that crosses it at right angles, and extends from above ears to the lower margin of the black throat; a small triangular curved black patch beneath the eye; the brown color of head is separated from the white by a nar-row black line ; the white, on side, and fore-neck, is margined beneath by a rather broad black band ; upper parts, reddish brown, barred with black, and streaked with buff; secondaries, pale purplish gray, spotted with black; primaries, dark brown, the outer webs spotted with white; sides of breast and flanks, dark plumbeous, almost black, spotted with white; line through middle of breast, and the belly, dark chestnut; rest of under parts and thighs, velvety black; maxilla, black; mandible, black, with yellowish spot on the side. Total length, 8¼ inches; wing, 5; tail, 2¼; tarsus, 1¼; bill, along culmen, ⅘.

Adult Female.—General color, light pinkish cinnamon, upper parts barred with black, more inclined to blotches, the bars frequently close together in places, and streaked with buff; head, without black or white stripes, barred on top and on crest with black; throat, pinky white; a few black spots on flanks, and lower parts of chest; abdomen and anal region, buff; secondaries, brownish black, barred with pale cinnamon; primaries, dark brown, spotted with white on outer webs; maxilla, black; mandible, pale horn color; claws, horn color. Total length, 8¾ inches; wing, 5; tail, 2¼; tarsus, 1¼. bill, along culmen, ⅝.

Young, about Half Grown.—Similar on upper parts to the female; throat and chin, pure white; under parts, brownish white, spotted with blackish brown, and streaked with buffy white; some black feathers appearing among the brown on the anal region; top of head rich brown, barred with black, and streaked with buffy white along the shaft ; wings, pinkish cinnamon, streaked with white, and occasional blackish bars across the feathers; primaries, as in the adult. Bill, light horn color.

Downy Young.—Head, pale brown; becoming gradually whitish on the throat, the occiput with a broad patch of chestnut; a blackish streak behind the eye; upper parts rusty brownish, indistinctly spotted with dusky, the rump bordered along each side by a whitish stripe; lower parts nearly uniform dull white.—*Ridgway.*

RUFFED GROUSE.

THIS well-known game bird, the Birch Partridge of certain portions of the British Provinces, Partridge of the Northern Atlantic States, and Pheasant of Virginia and the more Southern States, is distributed throughout the eastern portion of the Union from Massachusetts to Georgia and westward in the wooded regions of Ohio, Michigan, Wisconsin, and Minnesota to the Dakotas. North of Massachusetts it intergrades with its subspecies, the Canadian Ruffed Grouse, and it is not always an easy task to decide as to which form specimens obtained within this range really belong. In the Southeastern States it is confined mainly to the mountainous parts, rarely descending into the valleys or lowlands.

The habits of this fine bird are pretty well known by all lovers of dog and gun, and its wary nature, exceeding cunning, and general ability to take very excellent care of itself cause it to be regarded as one of the most thoroughly game members of the feathered race. The male Grouse drums at all times in the year: in the spring as a defiance to his rivals or as a call to the hens to come and admire him as he struts in magnificent form upon his chosen log; and in summer and autumn, or even winter, as an indication of his lusty vigor and general satisfaction with himself. The sound heard on these occasions is like a deep muffled roll of a drum, even likened by some persons to low thunder, and has a great ventriloquial power. It is produced solely by the wings, and these are not permitted to touch the body. The

14. Ruffed Grouse.

cock, mounted upon some familiar log, which he has probably occupied for the same purpose more than one season, puffs out his feathers until he appears nearly double the ordinary size, and with head drawn backwards, tail fully expanded and spread over his back, the tufts on either side of the neck raised and pushed forward, and wings trailing on the bark, moves with a mincing, affected gait along the fallen tree. Suddenly he throws his body forward and stretches out his neck, and commences to beat the air with his wings, but does not touch his flanks. The beats are rather slow and spasmodic at first, and then the strokes quicken, growing faster and faster every moment, until the wings disappear, leaving to the eye nothing but a rufous blur in their place. The muffled tone, low at first, swells with the increased rapidity of the beats until, in a loud, solemn roll, it is borne through the neighboring woods. Suddenly the wings are stilled, the roll ceases, and the noble bird raises himself erect and listens intently, as if anticipating a reply; but as all is quiet and the woods give forth no echoing sound or answering challenge, he begins to strut again. There has been no answer to the male's vigorous expression of challenge or invitation, but if this action just described was performed in the springtime it would be more than likely that from out the recesses of a near-by thicket some modest, demure hen would be watching and admiring the pompous male as he executed the fantastic movements of his haughty parade. Gaining courage at length she steps from out her concealment and watches the proud male, who, seeing the first member of his harem has arrived, redoubles his efforts to make himself captivating in the eyes of this fair one. Occasionally it is quite another visitor that comes to the trysting place, in the shape of a rival, and then between the lusty birds a desperate conflict ensues, wherein, perchance, some blood and many feathers are scattered upon the ground. Some believe that the Ruffed Grouse is not polygamous, but I think all the evidence we have seems to prove that it is, and that the male has many wives if he can get them. He pays no attention to the brood and is never seen with them, nor with the hen during the period of incubation, and I believe she hides her nest from him as well as from all her other enemies.

This bird inhabits dense thickets, swamps, clumps of bushes, and similar situations affording concealment, and prefers a hilly country or one strictly mountainous covered with timber, and is rarely seen in the open unless in the vicinity of some leafy covert. It frequents the banks of streams when overspread by bushes growing thickly together, but also is found at times in rather open woods with little or no undergrowth. When flushed this Grouse rises with a tremendous whir, which can be heard for a long distance and sounds not unlike a subdued roll of thunder, and an inexperienced sportsman is apt to be greatly flustrated by it and pretty sure to miss the bird, no matter how fair a mark it presents. The flight is extremely swift and powerful, and can be maintained for a long way, and the bird exhibits wonderful dexterity in threading the tangled brakes and by the unnumbered trees and branches without touching any in his headlong course. No little cunning is displayed also, that shows the bird is wide-awake and anxious to provide for its own safety, for as soon as it is on the wing it places some tree or bush between it and its pursuer and keeps on, as it flies, multiplying the obstacles for a successful shot. It lies well to the dog, but when it flushes always darts away from the side opposite to the sportsman, no matter how advantageously he may think he has chosen his position, and puts the first tree between the gun and its body. Usually not many adult birds are found together, five or six perhaps, rarely more, and they never rise all at once, but two or possibly three together, followed by the others singly. As the danger to themselves approaches nearer, occasionally a bird will lie so close that it will permit the sportsman to pass it, and then suddenly bursts away from behind him. I have never noticed any apparent retention of the scent by this bird after alighting, as is the case with Bob White, although I must acknowledge that there have been times when, after carefully marking some spot where a Grouse was seen to alight, it was impossible to find the bird, even after the ground had been thoroughly gone over by good dogs. Where they go to on such occasions is a mystery which, however, only increases our admiration for their cleverness.

The nest of the Ruffed Grouse is merely a hollow scratched in the ground, usually in well-concealed spots, beneath some bush or log, or in a dense thicket, alongside some overhanging rock, or in the tangled top of some fallen tree or underbrush that lies matted together in a confused mass several feet deep. Again it is sometimes placed in quite open situations without any attempt at concealment whatever, showing a trusting and confiding disposition rarely found in this bird unless in districts where it is little or never disturbed. The hollow is lined with grass, leaves, needles from the pine tree, and similar materials, distributed in a rather careless way, and, on an average, perhaps ten eggs are deposited, of varying shades of buff dotted with different sized spots of a pale reddish brown color. Incubation commences about the beginning of May and lasts, generally, from three to four weeks, the last being more nearly the correct time. The

hen, neglected by the male, who is never seen near the
nest, is a very close sitter, and only leaves her eggs when
danger to herself is imminent, and even then declines
to go away to any distance, but loiters in the vicinity,
watchirg every movement of her enemy and returning
to her treasures at the first opportunity, even at times
taking the chances of being captured rather than leave
her charge too long uncared for.

As soon as they have broken through the shell the
young run about, comical little brown tufts of down, and
follow the mother, who teaches them to feed on insects
and worms, and it requires but little instruction before
they become adepts and, with much seeming curiosity,
try every object they meet with as if testing its edibility.
Their little wings are too feeble to bear them up, and
to escape from danger, which is indicated by the warning
shrill note of the hen, they skillfully hide under any
favorable object, or squat and remain motionless, and
so well do they harmonize with the color of the ground
or dead leaves that it is quite impossible to distinguish
them without a diligent search. At night the mother
gathers them under her and covers them with her wings
in the manner of the domestic fowl, and protects them
from the dew and rain, for a wetting is a serious matter
to the chicks and is usually fatal. When about half
grown they all roost on trees, in which the young are
sure to take refuge if alarmed; but once perched on the
branches they seem to consider themselves as quite removed from all danger, remaining motionless and gazing
earnestly at the intruder on their haunts. This must be
the result of an inherited instinct that teaches them to flee
from their ground enemies, from whom they are usually
safe when once among the branches of a tree, but why
there should not be a similar instinct to bid them beware

of enemies of the air, such as Hawks and Owls, it is difficult to explain, unless it is on the principle of doing one thing at a time, if it is to be done well. The adult Ruffed Grouse feeds on various kinds of nuts, acorns, all sorts of berries in their season (some of them even of the poisonous kind, such as the sumach), and wild grapes, and, when these fail, eats the foliage of many plants, such as wintergreen, buttercup, partridge berry, etc. In the winter the food consists mainly of buds of the apple, the two birches, and other trees.

The males of this species keep apart after the breeding season is over, joining the coveys toward winter. This species bears the cold well, its feathered coat, carried down the leg to the heel, affording ample protection against the severity of the weather. When the snow covers the ground, or during a snowstorm, this bird is in the habit of diving headlong into the drifts toward evening, where it remains frequently entirely covered up, warm and snug, during the night, and flying out again at daybreak. But if during the night a crust should form upon the snow the poor Grouse is imprisoned and frequently dies of hunger, as escape is impossible unless a thaw speedily comes.

Its flesh, as is well known, is white and tender, but in the late fall or winter becomes very bitter occasionally, on account of the bird having fed on the leaves of the alder, and to many persons is then quite poisonous. In spite of the persistency with which this Grouse is hunted, and the vast number yearly taken in snares, it is still quite plentiful in many parts of its dipersion, and it would be sad indeed if unbridled persecution and avarice should ever cause its extermination, for then would disappear one of the noblest game birds known in our land.

BONASA UMBELLUS.

Geographical Distribution.—Eastern United States and Southern Canada, from Massachusetts to Northern Georgia; Mississippi and Arkansas, and westward to the Dakotas.

Adult Male.—Upper parts varied with yellowish brown and gray, barred on head, neck, upper part of back and wings, with black and rufous; lower part of back and rump gray, interspersed with dark red, and ovate spots of pale buff, surrounded with black; conspicuous, rather broad, streaks of buffy white on scapulars and wing-coverts; primaries, grayish brown, outer webs barred with ivory white; upper tail-coverts, gray, mottled, and barred, with black; tufts of broad, lengthened feathers on either side of neck, black, tipped with light brown and metallic green; throat, buff, faintly barred with brown; lower parts, buff on the chest, white on remaining parts, barred with brown, darkest and most conspicuous on the flanks, and just beneath the throat; under tail-coverts, buff, barred with blackish and with a V-shaped white mark at tip; tail, gray or yellowish brown; sometimes rusty, mottled with black, and crossed by irregular buff bands, bordered above by black, and a broad, subterminal black band bordered above and below, with gray, mottled with black, the upper gray bar bordered above with a narrow black bar; legs, feathered to middle of tarsus; maxilla, black; mandible, horn color. Total length, about 16 inches; wing, 7½; tail, 6½.

Adult Female.—Not to be distinguished from the male, save she is slightly smaller, and has either very small neck tufts or none at all.

Downy Young.—Upper parts, chestnut, darkest on front and top of head; rest of plumage, light buff, darkest on sides of head, with a conspicuous black line from back of eyes, across ear-coverts; bill, pale yellowish.

15.   Oregon, or Sabine's Ruffed Grouse.

OREGON OR SABINE'S GROUSE.

THIS is the handsomest member of the genus which includes the Ruffed Grouse of America. It is found on the mountains between the Coast Range and the Pacific, from northern British Columbia to California. Wherever its habitat approaches or overlaps that of another member of the genus it intergrades with it, and breeds wherever found. It is a beautiful bird, its rich red plumage relieved by black markings, and the orange, red, black, and white under tail-coverts render it a very attractive object, alive or dead. It is very plentiful in certain parts of British Columbia, and it is difficult to find a more striking object than this bird as it walks sedately before you, flipping out, with quick repeated jerks, the feathers of the tail, occasionally spreading it out to the fullest extent, and elevating and depressing the crest of lengthened feathers on the head.

Great numbers are killed by the Indians, mostly snared, and brought into the towns and cities lying along the Fraser and other rivers, and to Vancouver Island. Its habits are like those of the Ruffed Grouse, and the males drum from some fallen log, and fight furiously in the pairing season, as has already been described. If the season is mild they begin to drum in certain localities on the Pacific Coast in January or February, and frequently at night. Whenever I have heard this solemn roll after dark, which then has a peculiar weird sound, I wondered at the bird's willingness to disclose its position at an hour when many of its most active enemies

were abroad and searching for just such a toothsome
morsel as a fat Grouse, and I pictured to myself his
appearance, as, holding an evening reception, he displayed himself to the admiring gaze of his hens, as in
all the pride of conscious power and possession he
strutted about in the moonlight upon his favorite log.
Well for him that his rolling call did not bring some
prowling Owl gliding on swift and noiseless wing, or
stealthy, keen-scented fox to sweep him out of the scene
and life together. The males fight like gamecocks, with
lowered head and outstretched necks, the feathers
ruffled and standing out in all directions. I doubt if
these battles ever terminate fatally to either combatant,
the weaker giving way to his conqueror and taking
refuge in flight, recuperating his energies and both his
wounded body and spirit in the quiet retirement of the
deeper woods.

Sabine's Grouse is never found in large flocks, but
each family keeps by itself, and they feed upon all kinds
of seeds, insects, berries, nuts, leaves, and buds, and the
flesh is white and palatable save in the winter, when it
is often bitter, occasionally flavored with turpentine from
eating the buds of the fir tree. Nidification takes place
from April to June, the time somewhat depending on the
locality, and the eggs range from six to ten, perhaps
occasionally exceeding the latter number. They resemble those of other Ruffed Grouse and vary in a similar manner, and the nest is the usual cavity in the
ground, lined with almost anything lying about, such as
dead leaves and grass, or needles of the spruce or pine.

It is a large bird, and possesses all the game qualities
of its race, but from the localities it frequents can be
rarely hunted with well-broken dogs satisfactorily.

BONASA UMBELLUS SABINI.

Geographical Distribution.—Coast range of mountains from Northern British Columbia to California.

Adult Male.—Upper parts, mostly dark, rusty chestnut, mingled with black blotches and mottling; rump and upper tail-coverts inclined to gray in some specimens; feathers of wings have a central streak of yellowish white; flanks, rusty, barred with black; tail, deep rust color, barred irregularly, with black, tipped with gray, and having a subterminal black band, above which is another bar of gray; under tail-coverts, orange, barred with black and V-shaped white mark at tip; feathers of thighs and tarsus, rusty. Total length, about 17½ inches; wings, 7½; tail, 6¼.

Adult Female.—Resembles the male.

CANADIAN RUFFED GROUSE.

THIS bird, a subspecific form of the Ruffed Grouse, ranges in the northern half of Maine, throughout Canada as far west as the New Caledonia district in British Columbia, and is also found in northern Idaho, Oregon, and Washington on the eastern slopes of the Cascade Range, but does not enter the coast districts. It is very numerous in the thick forests that still cover a large portion of the Dominion of Canada, and is usually quite tame and confiding in disposition. When a covey or single bird is met with, flying is rarely resorted to, at least at first; the Grouse either walking perhaps a little more rapidly in front or to one side, or else they mount upon the lower branches of a tree close at hand and, motionless, gaze at the intruder. If a number have perched on the branches of different trees, frequently the majority can be shot before the survivors take alarm and fly deeper into the forest. The usual way of hunting them in these woods is to go with a little dog, which, striking the scent of a Grouse, follows it up until the bird is flushed, and flies usually immediately to a tree, at the foot of which the dog barks frantically, jumping against the trunk, and in many ways exhibiting the excitement under which he labors at seeing the most desired one so near and yet so far. The attention of the Grouse is entirely taken up with the antics and noise of the dog, and pays no heed to the approach of her more formidable and deadly enemy, the sportsman, who at short distance, with either

10. Canadian Ruffed Grouse.

shotgun or rifle—very frequently the latter is used—knocks the bird off the limb. Should there be other Grouse perched in the near vicinity the report of the weapon does not frighten them, and the firing is continued until a number of birds are tossing upon the ground, and the remainder, at length realizing that so much noise means serious danger, betake themselves to more secure retreats. When the rifle is employed for this kind of shooting, it is *de rigueur* that the head alone should be cut off, and any marring of the body by the bullet is to be condemned, and the marksman adjudged to be more lacking in skill than if he had missed the bird altogether. This shooting away the head by a single ball is not such a difficult feat as it may seem; for, in the first place, the distance between man and bird is usually quite short, possibly averaging not over ten yards, and the bird does all it can to insure a successful shot by standing bolt upright, and, with its neck stretched to the fullest length, remains as if carved in stone. The habits of the Canadian Grouse are the same as its relative of the Eastern part of the United States, and the description of one will answer for both. On account of the wooded character of the country it inhabits, it is not as commonly shot over a dog " at point " as is the Ruffed Grouse, but in any favorable locality it would lie as well, flush and present as favorable a mark for the sportsman, and show as much dexterity in evading his shot, by placing trees between itself and the gun, as does its relative of more southern climes.

Like all gallinaceous birds this Grouse rises with a resounding whir-r of the wings, but, as is the case with all the species, it can also take wing and steal away without making the slightest sound whatever. It seems to be almost an act of volition on the part of the bird whether it shall herald its departure with a burst of thundering sound, or omit it altogether. The noise certainly serves for a moment to unsettle the nerves of its enemies, unless experienced and accustomed to its ways, and many a Grouse has preserved its life by the shock the thunder of its wings has given to the startled nerves of the novice in field sports. Like other members of the tribe this Grouse is very courageous in defending its young from any enemy. If its nest and eggs are discovered it usually slinks quietly away, remaining, however, in the vicinity; but if the hen has a young brood with her, she is utterly forgetful of self, and rushes to meet either man or beast, and endeavors to lure him by feigned lameness and other pitiful devices away from the spot, sounding at the same time the warning notes to the young to scatter and hide. It has been known in its frenzied anxiety to peck at a man's trousers, as if its feeble efforts could compel its huge enemy to flee. If the intruder should happen to be a fox or other quadruped there is a good deal of method displayed by the hen in her attempts to entice him away from her young, and although she may flutter and flounder about within a few inches of the animal's nose, she is very careful not to go quite near enough to be caught, but evades easily the desperate efforts the beast makes to spring upon her. And when she has succeeded in drawing her foe a sufficient distance away, she suddenly rises on sounding wings, and with swift flight returns to her brood, leaving her defeated pursuer foolishly looking about him and probably lamenting the loss of all earthly hopes and joys, in this case typified by the vanishing prospect of a much-desired meal. But one brood is raised in a season, and the period of incubation, nest, its composition and position, number, color, and marking of the eggs, all closely resemble those already described in the article on the Ruffed Grouse.

BONASA UMBELLUS TOGATA.

Geographical Distribution.—Northern New York, and New England, and in Northern Idaho, Oregon, and Washington in the United States, and throughout the Dominion of Canada, to the district of New Caledonia, in British Columbia.

Adult Male.—Upper parts grayer than in the typical style, the brown markings especially on lower back and rump very conspicuous, and the gray ovate spots rather broadly surrounded with black; upper tail feathers, dark bluish gray, mottled and barred with black; under parts hardly distinguishable from the typical Ruffed Grouse, though perhaps the bars on flanks are usually darker; tail, mostly gray, irregularly barred, and mottled with black, the median feathers inclined to a yellowish brown, and a subterminal black band; large tufts of feathers on each side of neck, smoke-brown edged with metallic green. Measurements about the same as those of *B. umbellus.*

Adult Female.—With the exception of the neck tufts, which are either wanting or very small, there is no difference observable in the plumage of the female. While the birds found within the limits of distribution given above may properly be considered as representing a well-marked race of the typical Ruffed Grouse, it is very doubtful if the ordinary observer would detect anything in their plumage to indicate that they were different from the more southern species, and would probably consider them as all of the same kind. Specimens vary considerably, and it is not always easy for the expert to recognize the present race; knowledge of the locality from which the bird comes being often essential for a determination of its identity.

GRAY RUFFED GROUSE.

ANOTHER subspecies of the Ruffed Grouse is the present bird, which dwells in the central Rocky Mountain region, from the valley of the Yukon in Alaska, through British Columbia, and Idaho, Montana, and western Dakota south to Colorado. It possesses a plumage of a gray color, and is somewhat smaller than its relatives. Like the other Ruffed Grouse it is not migratory, and where it is found there it resides and breeds. It is fond of resorting to dense thickets and undergrowth that flourishes so luxuriantly along the mountain sides, and on the banks of streams, ascending at times to the loftiest heights, having been met with at 10,000 feet of elevation. Its habits are similar to those of its relatives, and the nest and eggs resemble those of the species already described.

It differs from the other Grouse of the Eastern portion of the United States and Canada by the uniform gray of the ground-color of its plumage and by its gray tail. When writing my monograph of the Grouse I thought that a good character consisted in the fact that the terminal black bar on the tail did not include the middle feathers, but the presence of more abundant material than was then obtainable proves that this supposition was not well founded. At best it is only a race of very questionable value. This bird was found abundant in the vicinity of Behring Straits at the head of Norton Sound wherever the woods occurred. It is common at

Edwin Sheppard

17. Gray Ruffed Grouse.

●

various points on the Yukon, and feeds upon the spruce buds, which give a disagreeable flavor to the flesh.

BONASA UMBELLUS UMBELLOIDES.

Geographical Distribution.—Rocky Mountain Region from Colorado, through Western Dakota, Montana, Idaho, and British Columbia to the Yukon in Alaska.

Adult Male.—Upper parts, mostly gray, some chestnut and black markings upon the neck, upper back, and wings; pale gray spots upon rump, all the feathers vermiculated with black; neck tufts, black, with metallic green reflections; under parts, white and buff mixed, especially so upon the chest, crossed with brown bars, changing to black on the flanks; under tail-coverts, gray, mottled with black and tipped with white; tail, pure gray, narrowly barred and mottled with black, and a subterminal black band. Total length about 14½ inches; wing, 7¼; tail 6.

Adult Female resembles the male, and is without neck tufts.

DUSKY GROUSE.

THIS species and its two races are, next to the Cock-of-the-Plains, the largest Grouse in the United States. The three forms range from New Mexico in the south, to Sitka, Alaska, in the north, and grade into each other at different points of their dispersion. Various names, besides the one at the head of this article, such as Pine Hen, Blue, Pine, and Gray Grouse are applied to these birds, no particular one being confined to any especial form, but in several localities the same name is given to the different races. The present species, the Dusky Grouse of naturalists, ranges from southern Idaho, east to western South Dakota, and then through portions of Wyoming, Nevada, Utah, and Colorado, through the northern half of Arizona to the southern part of New Mexico. It is not found in California. It is essentially a bird of the high mountains, and ranges to the limits of timber, coming down in winter to perhaps an altitude of 2000 feet, and dwells mainly in the forests of the thick spruce and fir. Solitary in its habits it is frequently found alone or in small parties of perhaps half a dozen individuals, and is of a roving, restless nature, and delights in rough hillsides and mountain summits, frequently changing its abode. The food consists of leaves, berries, buds of the pines—resorting to these last only in winter when the snow is deep—insects of all kinds, especially grasshoppers, worms, and grubs. In the spring the male struts exactly like the Turkey Gobbler; puffing out his feathers, dropping the wings, spreading

18. Dusky Grouse.

and elevating the tail, and drawing the head toward the back, he steps gingerly along, overcome for the moment by the extent and force of his amatory feelings. He has another method also of declaring his love, which he employs when perched in the midst of some thick fir or spruce. At such times he inflates a small sac, covered by a bare skin on either side of the neck, until it is half as large as an orange and something like it in color, surrounded by a fringe of white feathers; and suddenly exhausting the air, emits a low, booming sound having a strange ventriloquial power, and which can be heard for a singularly long distance. If met with on the ground this Grouse immediately takes to a tree if any are in the vicinity, and remains motionless on its perch, watching keenly every movement of its pursuer. · It is very difficult to discover it when it is so *en garde*, and if, after much peering into the somber depths of the foliage and many contortions of the neck, one catches sight of the bird, it is aware of the fact at once, and plunges down the mountain side with a roar of wings and swiftness of flight that almost always carries him away in safety. The speed at which the bird travels and the brief momentary glimpses that are afforded of his passing form, give but a slight chance for a successful shot.

At times when there are any grain fields near its resorts, the Dusky Grouse will enter the stubble to pick up the scattered kernels, and then is often quite tame and unsuspicious. I do not consider it a very wild or shy bird, at least I have never found it so, but this may be because I have mostly seen it in retired localities, in the depths of the forest, or on high mountains, where the bird had probably been seldom molested by man. When suddenly started it flies off with great

rapidity, uttering a loud, cackling note, and if there are
several together, the noise they make at such a time is
very considerable.   The nesting season begins in May or
June, according to the elevation at which the birds may
be, and but one brood is raised in a season.   A depression is made in the ground by a fallen log, or beneath a
bush, or perhaps in thick grass, or it may be right in the
open without any concealment, and this is lined without
much care with grass or any material that can be pressed
down by the bird, and about eight eggs are deposited.
Sometimes this number is greatly exceeded, and then it
is a question whether they have not been laid by more
than one hen.   The eggs have a ground color varying
from a creamy white to a rather deep buff, dotted,
spotted, and sometimes blotched with chestnut or chocolate brown, and these markings are pretty evenly distributed all over the shell.   The female remains on the
nest for about three weeks, when the young appear.
The chicks are exceedingly pretty little creatures, very
active, running as soon as they leave the shell, and are
adepts in hiding at the first alarm.   The mother appears
to have the sole charge of their welfare, and clucks to
them in a similar manner as does the domestic hen to
her brood.   When frightened the young scatter in every
direction, and the old bird usually takes refuge in some
tree.   As soon as the chicks are sufficiently grown so as
to be able to fly, they also immediately take to the trees
if alarmed, but make no farther effort to escape, seeming
to believe they are quite out of danger as soon as they
have left the ground.   From the habit which these
birds have of remaining motionless on the branches
until sometimes the entire covey is shot or killed
with sticks, they have received the name of Fool
hen or Fool Grouse.   The flesh of this bird is white

and well-flavored, and sometimes individuals are met with that will weigh as much as three pounds and a half.

DENDRAGAPUS OBSCURUS.

Geographical Distribution.—Rocky Mountains from Southern Idaho, Montana, and Western South Dakota to New Mexico and Arizona.

Adult Male.—Forehead, dull rufous ; back of head brownish black, feathers tipped with rusty; in some specimens the top of head is all slaty gray like the back; back of neck and upper parts, blackish brown, vermiculated with lighter brown, and gray, sometimes coarsely mottled with the same, especially on the wings, which are occasionally blotched with black; scapulars streaked with white along the shafts to the tips; white space on sides of neck; throat, white, mottled with black; sides of head, black; lower parts, slate gray, mottled with brown upon the flanks, the feathers of which have streaks along the shafts, and terminal spots white; under tail-coverts, blackish brown, with subapical bar of gray, mottled and bordered with black and tipped with white; tail, rounded, black, and tipped with a broad gray band; primaries, dark brown, outer webs and tips, mottled with gray; legs covered to the toes with pale brown feathers; bill, horn color. Total length, about 20 inches; wing, about 9½; tail, 8; tarsus, 1¾. Weight, about 3 pounds.

Adult Female.—Upper parts, mottled with black and buff, these frequently taking the form of bars and blotches; feathers, usually tipped with white; wings, slaty brown or gray, barred and mottled with buff, central streaks and terminal points, white; primaries, dark brown; throat, mostly buff; sides and front of neck and chest, dark brownish gray, barred and tipped with buffy white, sometimes only a spot of white on the tip; rest of under parts, slaty gray, the flank feathers tipped with white and mottled with buff and black; central tail feathers, blackish brown barred with pale grayish brown, the bars mottled with blackish; rest of tail, black, slightly mottled with gray, and a gray band at tip. Total length, about 17 inches; wing, 8¾; tail, 6.

SOOTY GROUSE.

THIS race of the last species ranges through the northern Rocky Mountains from the southern Sierra Nevada in California to northern Alaska in the Coast Range. Like the Dusky Grouse the present bird is a mountain dweller and is found at altitudes of 9000 feet, descending in winter 6000 or 7000 feet lower. It is much darker than the Dusky Grouse and has a narrower band on the tail, while the female has a dark rusty wash on the upper parts of her plumage. In its habits it does not differ from the preceding species and haunts the dense spruce and fir forests, taking refuge in the dark foliage of the trees and remaining motionless. I have met with this bird on the very summit of the mountains in the Coast Range, above the forest, and where the only covering was stunted trees and small clumps of bushes. I was riding along such a place one morning, my horse picking his way carefully over the rocks and broken ground and winding in and out among the low trees and bushes that stood plentifully about, when I saw a covey of about eight individuals of this Grouse upon the ground a short distance in front of me. Although they saw me and my horse very well, and must have heard his iron shoes striking the stones long before we came into view, they were not at all alarmed but continued to feed, running about without the least concern. Dismounting, I advanced toward them, when they drew together and looked at me in a wondering kind of a way, and one or two flew up into a low tree that was near by, but no effort

19.   Sooty Grouse.

was made to escape. Drawing nearer, I fired at one as
he rose, when the rest took wing but flew only a short
distance before alighting, and then began to run. They
took wing again as I advanced, when I secured two more,
and with little trouble and being obliged to walk but a
short distance I shot all but one, and he, finding the place
altogether unhealthy, flew down the mountain side, after
I had fired several times at his companions, and escaped.
This was in the month of September, but snow had not
yet fallen, and berries of various kinds were plentiful on
the bushes and vines, affording ample food for the birds.
They were fat and in fine condition, and made a most
acceptable addition to our camp larder.

In the thick firs it is practically impossible to see these
birds, as they not only remain motionless, often squatting
close to the limb or to the trunk itself, but their dark,
sooty plumage helps very much to conceal them; so, if
one's eyes do light upon a bird, it is usually deemed to be
only a knot or a bunch of some kind attached to the limb
or trunk. The males have the same habit in the spring, as
that already described in the article on the Dusky Grouse,
of blowing up the yellow sac on the side of the neck, and
emitting a sound that is heard for a considerable distance, a sort of *boom*, and from its ventriloquial powers,
it is impossible to determine whence it comes, or where
the bird is located. At such times, could you catch
a glimpse of the performer he would present a curious
appearance, for his neck would be puffed out until it
seemed as large as his body, or as if he was suffering
from a severe attack of the goiter, while the head,
apparently reduced in dimensions, would be perched
upon these yellow globes, and the bright eyes, half closed
from the pressure below them, would be surmounted by
a conspicuous semicircle of brilliant orange. The air

exhausted in the globes, he would resume for a brief space his normal shape, although the skin on the neck would seem flabby and wrinkled, when he would again proceed to inflate himself out of shape. The courting season over these sacs shrink entirely away, and the bare place is covered over by the feathers of the neck.

The time of love-making, period of nesting, style, and position of the nest, and number and color of the eggs, are almost precisely the same as has been described in the article on the Dusky Grouse. In fact there could not well be any difference of consequence between birds so closely related as are the above-named species and the present race, for practically they are the same bird; the probable greater amount of moisture in the districts inhabited by the Sooty Grouse causes its plumage to assume a darker, more somber hue; a fact known to occur in the coloring of all animals which dwell in countries visited by a great amount of rainfall. A belief is entertained among some that these Grouse remain in a somnolent state during the winter, regaining their activity in the spring; not like the old tale of the swallows, that they buried themselves in the mud, but that they went to sleep somewhere in the tree tops—hibernated in fact among the obscure depths of the firs and spruce. No doubt they do pass much of the winter amid the thick foliage of these trees, but the birds are far from being asleep, though for hours during the severe weather they may remain immovable. At such times the snow is usually very deep, and all food obtainable from the ground is hidden from sight, and the Grouse subsist on the buds and leaves of the trees amid which they have taken refuge, and have very little occasion to come from out their chosen resorts. Even the water they may need can be obtained from the snow lying on the branches.

In size this bird equals the Dusky Grouse and like its relative does not migrate, unless ascending and descending lofty mountains at certain periods of the year can be called migrating, and breeds wherever found.

DENDRAGAPUS OBSCURUS FULIGINOSUS.

Geographical Distribution.—Coast Range of Mountains from California eastward to Nevada, Western Idaho to Northern Alaska.

Adult Male.—Above, brownish black, lighter upon the back of neck, which is more of a slate color, and mottled, especially upon the wings, about the tips of the feathers, with brown and pale gray; rump and upper tail-coverts, mottled also with the same; no white central streaks on the scapulars, nor any very distinct white space on the side of neck; throat and sides of face, usually black, with a few small white spots on the former; breast sooty black, grading into very dark slate on rest of under parts; under tail-coverts, black, with white tip and a gray subapical bar mottled with black; tail, black, with a dark gray band at tip. Total length, about 21 inches; wing, 9¼; tail 8.

Adult Female.—Resembles the female of *D. obscurus*, but is much darker in hue, with a good deal of dark rusty on the upper parts.

RICHARDSON'S GROUSE.

THIS bird, which is another race of the Dusky Grouse, inhabits the eastern slopes of the Rocky Mountains from central Montana northward, through the interior of British North America, and is known as Richardson's Grouse. It is almost precisely similar in plumage to the Dusky Grouse, but lacks the distinct gray band on the tip of the tail, or has it very slightly indicated. The tail seems to be more square at the tip, and the feathers are much broader. Wherever its habitat overlaps that of either of its relatives, such as in Wyoming and Idaho, the present bird intergrades with them. It inhabits the same kind of country, high mountains, and breeds wherever found in spring, and passes much of the autumn in the bottoms, along creeks where the cover is plenty and berries abundant.

This Grouse builds a nest similar to its relatives, if scraping a slight hollow in the ground can be called building, but the eggs are smaller, although marked and colored in the same way. It did not seem to me to be as numerous in the places it frequented as were its relatives in their habitats, and in certain portions of Montana I have rarely met with it, but in other sections, as in the Big Horn Mountains, it is common. Its habits do not differ from those of the Dusky or Sooty Grouse, and the description of these already given will suffice for this bird as well. In size it equals the others, and its flesh is as white and well-flavored.

Edwin Sheppard

20.   Richardson's Grouse.

DENDRAGAPUS OBSCURUS RICHARDSONI.

Geographical Distribution.—Eastern slopes of Rocky Mountains, from Northern Wyoming, and Southeastern Idaho to the Liard River, latitude 61 in British North America.

Adult Male.—In general coloration this race resembles the *D. obscurus*, or Dusky Grouse, but has a differently shaped tail, which is much more square, and without any distinct terminal gray band, merely an edging of pale brown; the feathers also are much broader than those of the other two forms. In dimensions there is little, if any, difference.

Adult Female.—A specimen of this sex, which belonged to my collection, and is now contained in the American Museum of Natural History, number 2901, while resembling closely the female of the Dusky Grouse on the upper parts, presents certain differences beneath : it is much lighter upon the throat, being a buffy white, speckled with brown, and there is a good deal of white exhibited on lower breast, and on the flanks, the feathers, which are slaty gray, being broadly tipped with this hue ; the abdomen is slaty gray, the feathers only edged with whitish. Tail has the median feathers broadly barred with buff, and all are edged with whitish, the ground color being brownish black.

CANADA GROUSE.

RANGING from the Pacific Coast at Kadiak in northwestern Alaska through the British Possessions to
the Atlantic Ocean, and from the Rocky Mountains eastward through the upper portion of the northern tier of
States in the Union, the Black Partridge, Spruce or
Canada Grouse as it is variously called, is one of the best
known, and, in the localities it frequents, one of the com-
monest members of the Family. It dwells in the tam-
arack swamps, or where the spruce and fir grow thickest,
and is tame and unsuspicious, permitting one to approach
within a few feet of it as it stands upon a limb or on the
ground, gazing at the intruder with fearless eye, perhaps
simply uttering a soft cluck, as it steps on one side to let
him pass. Many are caught by a noose fastened to the
end of a stick, the Grouse permitting this to be placed
around its neck without moving, when it is jerked off
its perch. I have seen birds push this noose aside with
their bills without changing their position, when through
awkwardness, or unsteadiness of hand on account of a
long reach, the noose had touched the bird's head but
had not slipped over it.

This bird does not migrate, in the real sense of the
term, but may change its locality on account of the lack
or abundance of food in particular places, and it seems
able to withstand the severest weather; finding ample
shelter and protection from cold and storms in the dense
foliage of the trees amid which it lives, and subsistence
from the buds of the spruce, about their only food in

21. Canada Grouse.

winter. The Spruce Grouse is found usually in small flocks consisting generally of one family, but also old males are frequently met with alone, and I have always regarded it as a bird that was rather fond of solitude. Frequently, even in autumn, when the nights were becoming frosty, and snow flurries would hide the sun by day, heralding the coming winter, I have seen an old male, in the recesses of a swamp, strut about with ruffled feathers and trailing wings, as if the air were balmy and mild and spring were at hand to awaken in his breast the all-controlling passion of love, instead of being near the freezing point. He may have been going over the performance to keep himself in practice, or to impress me, possibly, with a proper sense of his own importance, for all his movements were calm and dignified in the extreme, and there was not the slightest evidence of fear, or of his being in any way incommoded by such an unimportant event as my presence.

I have never known the Canada Grouse to assemble together in large numbers or " pack " as it is called in the Western States, and if this has ever happened, it would be, I should imagine, a very unusual occurrence, and a large number of birds would find it very difficult to obtain sufficient food in any one locality even for a day.

The mating season begins in April, sometimes in the far north May is the earliest month, and at this time the male appears to the greatest advantage, and no Turkey Gobbler, in all his magnificence of gleaming scarlet and gold, is a prouder creature than this small Grouse. He tries by every means in his power to attract attention to himself and gain the admiration of anybody that is looking at him, whether it be the object of his affections, the demure and quiet little hen, or perchance his mortal

enemy and persecutor, man. His head is drawn back and
the bright blood-red combs stand erect and stiff above
each eye; the feathers of throat and breast are raised
and puffed out, and the wings are lowered and slightly
open; while the outspread tail, occasionally closed with
a swift movement, is elevated above the body. In this
apparently uncomfortable but proud and striking attitude, the bird moves slowly about with mincing, jerky
steps, highly impressed with his own importance and the
imposing display he is making. Certainly, at such a
time he is a beautiful object and well worth seeing. He
has a method of drumming also that is peculiar to himself, and is effected in the following manner: When in the
act of strutting he suddenly flies upward but not very
high, keeping the wings moving at a very rapid rate, and
after holding himself stationary for a moment in the air,
descends again slowly to the ground. The drumming
sound is produced by the rapid movement of the wings.
I have seen certain Pheasants, of the genus *Euplocamus*,
drum in a somewhat similar manner, although they did
not rise from the ground entirely. The wings would be
beaten violently and rapidly for a few moments, and the
bird would be raised on to the tips of its toes, sometimes
the nails just touching the ground, but I never saw it
entirely quit the earth; and the noise made by the wings
was a low, deep rumbling with a strange ventriloquial
power, and although I was looking directly at the bird
during the performance, the sound appeared to come
from some place a long distance away rather than
directly in front of me.

The nest is a loosely arranged affair of grass, leaves,
and other slight material, placed under some drooping
branches of a spruce in the depths of a swamp. A
writer in the Forest and Stream, Mr. Bishop of Kent-

ville, Nova Scotia, described a trait of this Grouse in nest-building which I have never witnessed myself. He states that the hen, when leaving her nest, will pick up sundry articles, like straws, grass, leaves, etc., and throw them over her back toward the nest, and sometimes, misled by the trail, she will throw these things in the wrong direction, but as soon as she discovers this, she faces about and throws them again over her back toward the nest. Then, while she is sitting, she reaches out and draws all these different articles lying near toward her, and arranges them in such a manner that before the young appear the nest is quite a deep affair and surrounded by a neat border. The number of eggs is about a dozen, sometimes a few less, or even more, with a ground color varying from a pale to a reddish buff, spotted and blotched with marks of various sizes, of a reddish brown or burnt umber color. Occasionally an unspotted egg may appear, and in a large series there is a very great variation in both color and markings. Only one brood is raised in a season, and the chicks are exceedingly pretty creatures, buffy yellow, with pale brown back and wings and sundry black marks on other parts of the body. The mother shows great courage in their defense, fluttering close to anyone who approaches her brood, and will almost permit herself to be touched with the hand as she crouches with ruffled feathers, or stumbles along in front of the intruder on her privacy.

The flesh of this Grouse is dark, and in the winter becomes at times very bitter, and is never as well flavored as that of the various Dusky or Ruffed Grouse. Still it is not to be despised and is often a welcome addition to the camp larder, when the bracing air of the woods and healthful exercise have produced an appetite that requires no sauce to make the food palatable. The young are very active creatures and run with light feet over the moss that carpets the swamps which are their home. As soon as they can fly they keep much among the branches of the trees, and always immediately take refuge there, if disturbed when on the ground. In the summer and autumn the Spruce Grouse, or *Perdrix de la Savanne,* as it is called by the *Habitans* or French-Canadians, feed on berries and buds of various kinds, and at this time they are in the best condition for the table. The crop often contains numbers of small stones, swallowed as is the habit of all gallinaceous birds to assist digestion or grinding the food. It is a beautifully plumaged bird, and is one of the most attractive objects of the dark, gloomy, and usually silent woods of the far North. In the northern part of New York State this Grouse is scarce, but is more often met with in the New England States, especially Maine, while in the West it is common in the large forests of northern Minnesota, and increases in numbers as one proceeds toward the Arctic regions wherever the forests extend.

CANACHITES CANADENSIS.

Geographical Distribution.—From Kadiak, Alaska, through British North America to the Atlantic Ocean, and from the eastern slopes of the Rocky Mountains through the northern tier of States to the coast line of New York and New England.

Adult Male.—Upper parts, gray, barred with black: wings, usually light gray, mottled and barred with black and brown tips, with central white streaks on scapulars, widening at the tips; under parts, black, with a mottled black and white border to the throat, and many of the feathers, especially on abdomen, tipped with pure white; flanks, pale brown, with irregular longitudinal black lines, and white streaks along the shafts, broadening at the tips; under tail-coverts, black tipped with white; upper tail-coverts, black, mottled with brown and tipped with gray; bill, black. Total length, about 14¼ inches; wings, 7; tail 5.

Adult Female.—Upper parts, barred with gray, buff, and black, the latter predominating, the gray most conspicuous on lower back and rump, and buff or ochraceous predominating upon side of breast and flanks, the feathers of these parts having central streaks of white broadening at the tip, sometimes the entire tip being white. Abdomen, black, feathers tipped with white; under tail-coverts, black, barred with buff, and tipped with white; median tail feathers, barred with ochraceous and black; remainder black, with irregular narrow lines of ochraceous, chiefly on the outer webs, and tipped with ochraceous, widest on outer feathers. Dimensions about the same as those of the male.

Downy Young.—General color, lemon yellow, darkest on the breast, a black bar through the eye to nape; top of head and neck, back, and wings, rusty, with two spots on head, and transverse ones on wings, black; maxilla, black; mandible, pale horn color; feet, yellowish.

FRANKLIN'S GROUSE.

A TRULY Northern species, like its relative the Canada Grouse, this bird is found but in few localities in the United States, being more an inhabitant of the country lying above our border. It ranges from Washington and Oregon, through northern Idaho to the Belt Range in Montana, and north of our line, in British Columbia and the mountains of the Coast Range. In most parts of Alaska it seems to be supplanted by the Canada Grouse, which reaches the Pacific Coast in that Territory; but it is Franklin's Grouse that is met with in the mountains of the Coast Range in British Columbia.

My experience with this bird has been gained mainly in the last-named mountains, where I have met with it on various occasions. It inhabits similar localities to those frequented by the Spruce Grouse, and is equally tame and confiding, hardly taking the trouble to move out of the way of man or horse—perhaps mule would be a better term—and seems quite indifferent to the presence of intruders in its haunts. As a game bird it affords no sport whatever, and an entire flock can be killed before it enters the head of any of its members that it would be a wise thing to take wing and seek some more healthy locality. I have met flocks of this species, perhaps consisting of eight or ten individuals, dusting themselves in the trails crossing the mountains, or scattered about them on either side, and could easily have bagged the entire lot

22. Franklin's Grouse.

without creating an alarm, or causing the birds to make any attempt at flight. Of course nothing but the necessity of obtaining food for the camp would excuse such thorough slaughter, for certainly there was no sport in shooting creatures that would not get out of the way, nor rarely make an attempt to fly, and it seemed a pity to kill birds for the pot that were so rare in all ornithological collections. A pair obtained on one of these occasions, I am glad to think, is now in the collection of the American Museum of Natural History in New York. The males of Franklin's Grouse are like their relatives of the other species, pugnacious creatures, attacking almost anything, and very fearless. This trait is of course exhibited chiefly during the mating season, but they are quite ready to act on the offensive or defensive at any time. They have also the same habit as the Spruce Grouse of erecting the feathers just below the head, making the birds appear very odd, and the males strut in a similar way as that already described in the article on the other species. This Grouse appears not to go far from water, and when in the forest, if not in precisely a swamp, the birds would always be found in some wet spot, or near a brook or spring.

Franklin's Grouse is a thorough mountaineer, living at altitudes varying all the way from 5000 to 10,000 feet, and it is only occasionally that it descends much below the first-named elevation. Wherever found there it resides and breeds, raising the young brood probably in the same locality where the parents themselves grew to maturity. It is not rare in the places it frequents, but is often met with in considerable numbers; not in large flocks, but numerous coveys scattered over a considerable area. From its trustful nature and consequent reluctance to save itself by flight, a great many are killed both by Indians and whites, and large numbers are obtained by hitting them with sticks and stones, at throwing which the Indians are very expert. The nest of this species resembles that of the Canada Grouse, merely a shallow depression in the ground or moss, lined with leaves or grass, and the eggs resemble exactly those of its relative, but are slightly smaller. A single brood is raised in a season, and nesting commences the latter part of May or beginning of June. This species and the preceding one are very much alike in the general color of their plumage, but Franklin's Grouse can always be recognized by the broad white bars at the end of the upper tail-coverts, and the tail itself is without the white edging, and more inclined to a square shape or one only slightly rounded. In size the two forms are about equal.

CANACHITES FRANKLINI.

Geographical Distribution.—Rocky Mountains from Northwest Montana, through Oregon and Washington, and the coast range of British Columbia to Alaska.

Adult Male.—Upper parts, similar to the Spruce Grouse, but with the upper back, scapulars, and wings of a brown hue, the bars and mottling being of that color; no white central streaks on the wings, but some of the tertials tipped with white; upper tail-coverts very broadly tipped with white, and this is a conspicuous character of this species; the entire under parts are like those of its Eastern relative, but the white beneath and on the sides of the throat is narrower and much less prominent; tail, almost square, and of a uniform sooty brown, nearly black on the apical half; bill, black. Total length, about 15¼ inches; wing, 7¼; tail, 5.

Adult Female.—Upper parts, gray, barred with black and ochraceous, narrowest on head and neck, broadest and most conspicuous on upper part of back; upper tail-coverts ochraceous, mottled with black and tipped with white; innermost secondaries with a central line and tip, white; primaries, dark brown;

outer webs, mottled with light brown; under parts, barred with black and ochraceous, feathers tipped broadly with white upon the flanks and belly; under tail-coverts, black, barred with orange and tipped broadly with white; tail, ochraceous, barred and mottled with black and tipped with white; thighs and tarsi, ashy brown; bill, black. Measurements about as in the male.

PRAIRIE HEN.

THROUGHOUT the prairies of the Mississippi Valley, south to Louisiana and Texas and west to Kansas and Dakota, east to Indiana and Kentucky and north to Manitoba, this familiar and well-known bird is found in greater or less abundance. Along the eastern limit of its dispersion the Prairie Chicken is rapidly diminishing, and like the buffalo, and many other wild creatures that once roamed in countless numbers over certain portions of our land, will doubtless soon entirely disappear. But as if to atone for the loss of its eastern possessions, it follows its star of empire westward, and as the settlements increase and multiply, so the Prairie Hen appears to flourish, and like Bob White accompanies man as he penetrates the wilderness, either of forest or treeless plains. It is a resident species throughout nearly all its range, breeding where found, save in the northern portions of our land, and in the autumn, when the weather is severe, the females, for the flocks are mostly of that sex, leave the northern limit of their habitat and proceed south to more genial climes, such as may be found in Iowa and Missouri. In the spring, as soon as the weather has become somewhat settled, the birds all return to their northern homes. The males seem to remain behind, whether too lazy to undertake the journey, or less mindful of the excessive cold frequently experienced near the Canadian border, it is difficult to determine, but probably the cold affects them less.

Edwin Sheppard

23. Prairie Hen.

At one time this bird was dispersed over a large part of the eastern United States, and was by no means especially a prairie dweller, but it is difficult to ascertain where its limits and those of the Heath Hen, now restricted to Martha's Vineyard, originally were, but probably somewhere along the boundaries of the Middle States. I do not imagine the Heath Hen was more of a woodland species than is the Prairie Chicken, but both dwelt among the open woods if there were any within their range. In the spring, in the early mornings, throughout the country which this species inhabits, soon after daybreak, is heard the loud booming of the males, when, assembled upon some slight elevations in the prairie, they inflate and exhaust the yellow sacs on either side of the neck, producing, as the orange-colored bladder collapses, a low, booming sound that can be heard for a long distance. The lengthened feathers on the neck at such times are elevated and projected stiffly forward, almost meeting above the head. When their sacs are fully extended the bird has a most comical appearance, as his head nearly disappears between the enormous globes which stand out in either side until his neck has as large a diameter as his body. The tail is raised above the back and spread out to its fullest extent, and the wings are lowered with the primaries scraping along the ground. In this uncomfortable attitude the male struts before the females, who at first take but little interest in the exhibition and hardly deign a glance at their adorer, striving so hard to appear magnificent and attractive. He makes a sudden rush forward, darting fiery glances from his eyes, peering out from beneath the neck feathers, anxiously watching the effect his striking appearance is having upon the fair ones, and then, lowering his bill toward the ground and spreading the mandibles, he exhausts the air sacs and gives vent to the booming sound that rolls and echoes, like the tones from the great pipes of the organ, over the wide prairie. Where hundreds of males are so occupied in the stillness of the early day, before the sun has risen, and the shadows of departing night are being faintly dissipated by the rosy tints that herald his coming beams, the concert of varied sounds is very impressive, as the many different tones come from every direction, echoing through the air, and carried in strong booming notes for great distances over the prairie-land. Shortly after the sun has fairly risen the display ceases and the birds go about their daily avocation, to commence the same exhibition again the next morning. Occasionally during the day, in places where the birds are not molested, or removed from the presence of human beings, the *boom* of some male may be heard at almost any hour, but no concerts are attempted save just at daybreak. These displays continue for a number of days, and toward the latter part of their courtship the males are more anxious, and do not take as much care to avoid contact with each other as they did at first, and then desperate battles occur, the fighting cocks leaping into the air and tearing at each other with bills and claws and striking with their wings, until the weaker, utterly exhausted, flees away and leaves the field and, what is of much more importance doubtless in his eyes, the hens also, to the victor.

These fair feathered creatures have lately shown much more interest in the antics and combats of the males, and move about them, quickly at times, or else remain motionless and watch them displaying themselves in all the pride of conscious power and beauty as they slowly move along, or when, in the midst of the deadly fray, the courageous birds strive for some particular sweetheart beloved by both combatants. Having chosen their mates the pairs seek suitable places for the nest, which is placed in the midst of thick prairie grass, or in a corner of some field among weeds, on the borders of swamps, in cultivated grounds, or far out on the open prairie, sometimes in quite exposed situations. A slight depression in the soil is lined with grass and some feathers from the hen's own body. Prairie fires, mowing machines, and floods destroy many thousands of eggs in a season, and occasionally the young themselves are caught and slain by the sharp knives that are laying low the grass. The usual number of eggs is from ten to fourteen, but sometimes twenty or more have been found in one nest. Their color shades from a pale cream to light brown, regularly spotted with fine reddish brown dots, and there is great variation among them, no two being exactly alike. Incubation lasts from twenty-three to twenty-eight days, and one brood is raised in a season, though, if the eggs be destroyed or lost from any cause, the hen may lay again, but this is exceptional. The male does not trouble himself with the cares of either the nesting or of the young when they appear, but keeps to himself, and the broods probably get along just as well without him.

As soon as they are hatched the chicks leave the nest, and the female leads them away where insects, especially grasshoppers, abound, and these at first are their sole food. As they grow in size and strength they eat grain of different sorts as they may happen to find it, and also berries. The hen is courageous and protects her brood to the best of her limited ability, feigning lameness and employing all the usual artifices to attract attention to herself and give her little ones a chance to escape. These hide away with great celerity and adroitness, and it is often extraordinary, how easily the chicks will disappear from view and effectually escape all search, be it carried on ever so patiently and perseveringly, even on the open prairie with apparently no opportunities for concealment. Towards the end of August the broods are nearly full grown, and later in the season many flocks pack together until several hundreds are present in one gathering. They are then usually very wild, and, when started, will fly often several miles before alighting, and little can be done with them over dogs. But before this congregating together takes place the Prairie Chicken lies well to the dog, and is one of the most desirable of the game birds as an object of sport in the field.

A covey having been located by the dog, the birds will almost always lie very close, flushing in easy range in twos or threes, and after, as may be supposed, all the birds have either flown away or rest in the sportsman's game bag, there is always still one old bird remaining, which rises at length with a prodigious fluttering and cackling, either just when the sportsman is reloading his gun and so escapes, or else, having miscalculated his time, appears when the guns are all ready for him, and joins his brethren in the pocket or wagon. When young, the flesh of the Prairie Hen is white, but becomes dark as the bird attains its full growth. It is excellent for the table, especially when eaten soon after the bird is killed, for it loses flavor after having been kept for a length of time, especially if, as is the case with thousands of birds served in the Eastern cities, they have been frozen, tossed about perhaps for weeks like lumps of ice, and then thawed out before being cooked. The most toothsome morsel in the world, after such treatment, could not be expected to have much more flavor than a dried chip.

When flushed the Pinnated Grouse always utters a few clucks, and the crest on the head is frequently raised. It has the habit of lifting and depressing the crest when walking on the ground and when one approaches near to it. This is only, however, when it has not been much disturbed and is tame. At other times it crouches among the grass or close to the ground, and only moves to take wing. In spite of the enormous number killed every year by all sort of means, the species still manages to hold its own fairly well in many localities, but the inevitable day will surely come that will bring the same fate to all our wild creatures, and the Prairie Chicken, like other natives of the wilderness, will remain only as a memory.

TYMPANUCHUS AMERICANUS.

Geographical Distribution.—Prairies of Mississippi Valley from Manitoba on the northeast to Ontario, Michigan, and Ohio, west to the Dakotas, Kansas, and the Indian Territory, and south to Louisiana and Texas.

Adult Male.—Upper parts, brown, barred with black and buff; wing feathers, tipped with buff; a tuft of stiff, elongated feathers, capable of being elevated over the head on either side of the neck, black, with buff centers, frequently chestnut on the inner webs; chin, throat, and cheeks, buff; the latter marked with dark brown spots; a brown line from mouth, beneath the eye to ear-coverts; buff stripe from maxilla to and beyond the eye; under parts, white, barred with brown or blackish brown; flanks, barred with blackish brown, and buff; under tail-coverts, white, edged at tip with brown and margined with dark brown and buff; tail, brown, darkest on median feathers, and tipped with white; large sac of loose skin, capable of inflation beneath the long neck feathers. Total length, about 18 inches; wing, 9; tail, 4¼.

Adult Female.—Resembles the male, but is without the neck sac, has the neck tufts very short or rudimentary, and the tail feathers have numerous distinct bars of buff. Total length, about 17¼ inches; wing, 8¾; tail, 3¾.

In the breeding season there is a red skin over the eye, large and erectile in the male.

Downy Young.—General color, yellowish buff, inclined to rusty on breast and sides; several spots or broken lines on head and occiput, stripe across shoulder, and blotches on back and rump black, wing feathers barred with light brown and buff, and striped in center with white.

Edwin Sheppard.

24. Heath Hen.

HEATH HEN.

MARTHA'S VINEYARD, an island off the coast of Massachusetts, is the last stronghold of the Heath Hen, which formerly dwelt in various parts of that State, as well as in Connecticut, on Long Island, on Hempstead Plains, and other localities, New Jersey, and Pennsylvania. It may also have ranged over a greater part of the Middle States. It closely resembles the Pinnated Grouse of the Western States, and it would require an expert to distinguish readily the points of difference between them. But still in coloring, shape of the lanceolate neck feathers of the male, short tarsus, and generally smaller size, it has sufficient differences to be classed as a distinct species.

The Heath Hen is, now at all events, a woodland bird and dwells among the almost impregnable tracts of scrubby oaks and pines which cover perhaps an area of forty square miles, and comprise about all the wooded portion of Martha's Vineyard. Within this limited area several hundred birds are assembled, the last remnant of the great host that at one time was spread over a number of the Atlantic States. The nature of the coverts they frequent, difficult for man to penetrate, and their habit of remaining almost continually in the thick woods, insures that protection which will probably preserve the species, even in its diminished numbers, for a long time to come. Living thus almost entirely in these woods of scrub oaks, the birds feed on the acorns that lie scattered over the ground, occasionally wandering out into the open to seek for grain, berries, or leaves which afford them a slight change of diet, and sometimes in winter, when the weather is severe and the snow deep, they will approach the barns or other buildings on the farms, and pick up whatever they can find in the way of grain or other suitable food. The nesting season appears to be a late one, although this is difficult to determine, as but few persons have seen the nest, but young broods have been met with late in July, which would show that incubation must have commenced somewhere near the beginning of that month. The booming note of the males is heard in the spring when they commence their courting, between daybreak and sunrise, and although, on account of the nature of the ground, the birds are seldom seen, yet the antics they practice at that time may not vary from those of the Pinnated Grouse at the same season. This bcoming sound at all events is very similar to that made by the Western birds. The eggs have rarely been taken, but a set of six, in the possession of my friend Mr. William Brewster of Cambridge, are about the same size as those of the Pinnated Grouse, perhaps a little smaller, and buffy white or creamy buff in color, tinged with greenish and unspotted. The nest is the usual slight depression in the soil, carelessly lined, and situated among weeds or anything affording concealment, and placed near a stump, roots of a tree, or fallen log.

With adequate protection from strictly enforced laws, aided by the stunted trees and bushes forming a tangled growth and covering the ground they frequent, there is no reason why these survivors of a disappearing race should not be able to preserve the existence of the species through long series of years yet to come.

TYMPANUCHUS CUPIDO.

Geographical Distribution.—Island of Martha's Vineyard, Massachusetts. Formerly abundant on Long Island, New Jersey, Eastern Pennsylvania, and Virginia, but now extinct in all those localities.

Adult Male.—Closely resembling the previous species, but distinguishable by its short pointed neck feathers, the tufts composed of not more than ten lanceolate feathers (those of *T. americanus* containing more than this number), and by the large terminal whitish buff spots on the scapulars. Length of wing, about 8½ inches; tail, 4.

Female has the lanceolate neck feathers rudimentary, and is slightly smaller than the male.

LESSER PRAIRIE HEN.

A SMALLER, pale-colored variety of the Pinnated Grouse, inhabiting southwestern Kansas, the western part of Indian Territory, and western Texas, has been designated as a separate race under the name given above. . It would not probably be regarded as in any way different from the Pinnated Grouse by one who was not an ornithologist and trained to observe technical or slight distinctions between animals. It is somewhat different in coloring and appears smaller, though measurements seem to show that the size of the two birds is pretty nearly equal. In certain parts of Texas, such as the districts lying to the south and southeast of San Antonio, this race is very abundant, and is also found, but in more limited numbers, north of that city. It is also common in the Indian Territory. Its most southern range in Texas appears to be just north of Fort Brown, near the coast. The eggs are somewhat smaller than those of the Northern Prairie Chicken, and paler in color, being a creamy or buffy white, covered with very fine grayish or brownish dots; sometimes the shell is entirely unspotted. The habits and nesting of this race are practically not different from those of the species already described.

TYMPANUCHUS PALLIDICINCTUS.

Geographical Distribution.—Western Texas, through Indian Territory to Kansas.

Adult Male.—Differs from the Pinnated Grouse in being much

25. Lesser Prairie Hen.

darker above, and barred by light brown or buff, inclosed between two black bars, as is also the case on the flank feathers; the brown bars on the pale brown under parts are narrow and close together, especially on the breast; under tail-coverts, barred with dark brown and white, and tipped with white; neck tufts, broad, and feathers rounded at tip; loose skin beneath neck tufts. Total length, about 15 inches; wing, 8¼; tail, 4.

Adult Female.—Like male, without air sacs on neck, and rudimentary neck tufts; tail barred with rusty. Wing, 8 inches; tail, 3⅞.

ATTWATER'S PRAIRIE HEN.

THIS is another race of the Northern species, and appears to be restricted to the coast line of Louisiana and Texas. It differs from the other species of the genus in having the tarsus feathered only on the upper two-thirds, and a suffusion of cinnamon rufous on the tufts of long feathers in the neck, which are almost square at their tips, forming almost a collar in front at base of neck. In size it is about the same as *T. pallidicinctus.*

TYMPANUCHUS ATTWATERI.

Geographical Distribution.—Gulf coast of Texas and Louisiana.

Adult Male.—Similar to *T. americanus,* but much darker on the back and top of head; neck tufts, black on tips and apical half of outer webs, remainder, buff and cinnamon rufous; base of neck in front and on sides, cinnamon rufous, with central buff stripes on feathers, broadening toward the tips; throat and fore-neck, pale buff spotted with brown; tail, smoky-brown, whitish buff on margins of outer webs; tarsi, feathered on upper two-thirds. Total length, 15 inches; wing, $8\frac{1}{10}$; tail, 3.

Adult female smaller. Total length, $13\frac{3}{4}$ inches; wing, 8; tail, 3.

Downy Young.—Upper parts, pale chestnut; spot on top of head, and broken line on occiput, and indistinct lines on back, wings, and rump, black; rest of body lemon yellow, with a rusty tinge on breast

Edwin Sheppard.

26.   Attwater's Prairie Hen.

27. Sharp-Tailed Grouse.

SHARP-TAILED GROUSE.

THERE are three races of Sharp-tailed Grouse: a dark form, almost black in its markings, and two lighter colored subspecies. The present is the dark style and has a high Northern dispersion, never coming within the boundaries of the United States. It ranges throughout British America as high as 69° of north latitude, and does not come to the south much below 52°. It has not been found west of the Rocky Mountains, but occurs on some of the eastern slopes, is abundant near Great Slave Lake, and on the Atlantic side of the continent is not uncommon around Hudson Bay.

Mr. MacFarlane has given about all the information we have of this species in its native haunts, and he says it breeds in the pine forests on both sides of the Lockhart and Anderson rivers, where some nests were taken. A single brood is raised in a season, and its habits and economy do not differ from the better known birds living within the limits of the Union. The number of eggs ranges from seven to fourteen, of a fawn or very dark buff color, or olive-brown marked with small spots of reddish brown. The eggs are much darker in appearance than those of either of the subspecies, and, like those of many of the other species of Grouse, the markings can be easily rubbed off, leaving the shell a pale hue, sometimes almost white. Incubation begins very early, before the snow and ice have vanished in those northern regions, and nests with eggs have been found as early as the beginning of May. It dwells both in the wooded districts and in the open country, and from the striking contrast between the black and white of its plumage presents a very handsome appearance. The legs are very heavily feathered and the feet also, the toes being completely covered to the claws, thus affording ample protection to the bird against the intense cold of the Arctic regions in which it lives.

Between the typical style of the Sharp-tailed Grouse and that of the Columbian Sharp-tailed Grouse there is exhibited in the birds living on our Northern borders and some distance beyond, every gradation between the dark Arctic birds and the light-colored ones of the United States, so that it is impossible to fix any precise limit to the habitat of either form. It can only be stated that, as the United States form goes northward it gradually, by successive degrees, darkens into the typical Grouse of the Arctic regions, having no especial locality where the divergence commences. In size it is about the same as the Columbian Grouse, and doubtless its flesh is equally palatable.

PEDIŒCETES PHASIANELLUS.

Geographical Distribution.—British America from Lake Superior and Hudson Bay to Fort Simpson.

Adult Male.—Top of head, neck, and entire upper parts, black, barred and mottled everywhere except on top of head, with buff, the bars narrow, thus making the prevailing color black, instead of brown or buff; the bars are pale buff on rump and upper tail-coverts, giving these a lighter appearance than the rest of the upper parts; wings, like the back, with broad, central white streaks on the scapulars, and white spots on the coverts and white bars and tips to the secondaries; primaries, dark chocolate brown, with equidistant white spots on outer webs; under parts, white, spotted with black on the throat and front of neck, and broad V-shaped blackish brown marks near the center of the feathers, most numerous upon the breast and flanks, and growing gradually smaller and fewer as they approach the abdomen; central elongated feathers of the tail, black, irregularly barred with white and light buff, remainder of feathers, white; under tail-coverts, white, with a dark brown line along the shafts of some of the feathers. Legs and toes, covered with hairy light brown feathers; bill, blackish brown. Total length, about 16 inches; wing, 8½; tail, to end of median feathers, 5¼.

Adult Female.—There does not seem to be any particular difference in the coloration of the sexes, but the female may be slightly smaller.

COLUMBIAN SHARP-TAILED GROUSE.

INHABITING the Northwestern States of the Union from Montana and Wyoming to Washington and Oregon, on the eastern slopes of the mountains which there check its progress toward the Pacific, and thence north through British Columbia to Alaska, this bird is the Western representative of the race dwelling upon the prairies of the States lying just east of the Rocky Mountains. South it goes to Nevada and the northeastern part of California. To most persons the two forms here distinguished as the Columbian and Prairie Sharp-tailed Grouse would appear to be the same, the slight differences of color and style of markings not being sufficiently striking and tangible to be perceived without having the assistance of an expert to point them out. And, in truth, the differences are very slight, but nevertheless have been deemed important enough to give the birds the rank of separate races. The locality of a specimen, however, would be of the highest importance, in many instances, in assisting the decision as to which race it belonged. This Grouse, known, in addition to the name given above, as the Pin-tail, Spike-tail Grouse, and Prairie Chicken, has practically the same habits as those of its Eastern relative, and is very common throughout the districts in which it is found. Like the Prairie Sharp-tail, it keeps to the open country, and if met with in summer in the wooded portions, it will only be along their edges, where it has easy access to the prairie-land.

In the spring, before sunrise, these birds meet together

28. Columbian Sharp-Tailed Grouse.

and "dance" in a similar way to that described in the article on the Pinnated Grouse, although, if possible, they are more active in their movements and exhibit greater excitement. This "saturnalia" is preparatory to selecting mates for the serious business of the approaching nesting season, and the males make the most frantic efforts to cause themselves to appear attractive to the numerous hens gathered around. They have, like the Pinnated and some other Grouse, a loose skin on the sides of the neck, capable of being inflated, swelling out like two great oranges, one on either side, which emit, when being exhausted, a sound that has been likened to a "bubbling crow," quite different to the organ-like "boom" of the Prairie Chicken. Incubation begins the latter part of April, the nest being placed in a bunch of grass, well concealed from view, and consists of a depression lined with grass and occasionally some feathers from the hen's abdomen. On this are deposited from ten to fifteen eggs, pale buff or brown in color, covered with very fine reddish brown spots. In about three weeks the young appear, active little creatures running about as soon as they are freed from the shell, and are carefully watched and tended by the hen, who is always ready to guard and defend them with great courage and determination. Like the young of all Grouse, insects are the principal means of subsistence at this early period of their lives, and later they feed on seeds, leaves, and berries. Toward September the young are pretty well grown, and later they pack, assembling in large flocks, and are then usually wild and difficult to approach. In certain parts of their dispersion they resort to swamps and near-by woods. In winter they frequently retire to the timbered country, probably as a refuge from severe storms and deep snows, and at this time may often be seen perched on trees. I think, however, this is a common habit of all Sharp-tailed Grouse if they happen to be in a country where trees abound, and it is a very usual occurrence in winter, or early in the morning during the autumn, to see numbers of Grouse standing or sitting upon the branches. When flushed they always cackle as they rise, and fly swiftly in a straight line, alternately sailing along and then flapping the wings with a few quick, short strokes. They are able to go long distances without stopping, but, as a rule, when not much hunted, they alight after making a short flight. As the country becomes settled this Grouse is more seldom met with, as it retires to the wilder portions of the land, for, unlike the Pinnated Grouse, it is a bird of the wilderness and shuns man's habitations.

PEDIŒCETES PHASIANELLUS COLUMBIANUS.

Geographical Distribution.—Eastern Rocky Mountains, from Montana and Wyoming to Oregon and Washington, then northward west of mountains to Central Alaska.

Adult Male.—Upper parts, grayish buff, with but a little of the rusty hue (this, if present, confined to the middle of the back), and barred, mottled, and occasionally blotched with black; the white markings and spots on scapulars and wings not so conspicuous as in the previous species, when contrasted with the hue of the general plumage; throat and sides of face pale buff, with a cluster of brown spots on the cheeks; breast, light buff, rest of under parts and flanks, white, all with longitudinal lines of blackish brown, sometimes rounded at the tip, sometimes inclined to a V-shape; lengthened central tail feathers, like the rump, lateral ones grayish white, barred with blackish brown, especially on outer webs; under tail-coverts, white barred with blackish brown, chiefly on the outer webs ; legs, covered to the toes with brownish white feathers ; maxilla, horn color ; mandible, brownish white. Total length, about 15½ inches; wing, 7¾; tail, 4½.

Adult Female.—Closely resembles the male, but the central tail feathers barely extend beyond the lateral ones.

29. Prairie Sharp-Tailed Grouse.

PRAIRIE SHARP-TAILED GROUSE.

THIS race of the Sharp-tailed Grouse ranges from Montana on the north to Wisconsin and Illinois on the east, Colorado on the west, and New Mexico on the south. This is practically its present distribution, but doubtless long ago its eastern limit was much nearer to the Atlantic Coast than it is now, but the bird was forced westward by the advance of civilization and settlement of the country, and its place occupied by the Pinnated Grouse, which follows man's footsteps as he penetrates into the wilderness. This process is indeed going on to-day, and yearly the range of the Sharp-tailed Grouse is becoming more restricted as it is hemmed in by settlements from every side. Although it is generally regarded as exclusively a prairie bird, this is a mistaken idea, as has been shown in the account of the Northern and Western forms, which do in certain localities frequent the woods, and there is no reason whatever to suppose that in earlier times these birds were not as much at home, and throve as well in forest-covered districts, as did the Prairie Chicken at one time, when it was abundant on large tracts of the Atlantic Coast, or as the remnant left does to-day on Martha's Vineyard.

The habits of this well-known bird do not differ from those of the Western race already described, nor indeed from those of the Pinnated Grouse. In the early spring, in the month of April, when perhaps in many parts of their habitat in the northern regions, the snow still remains upon the ground, the birds, both males and females, assemble at some favorite place just as day is breaking, to go through a performance as curious as it is eccentric. The males with ruffled feathers, spread tails, expanded air sacs on the neck, heads drawn toward the back, and drooping wings (in fact the whole body puffed out as nearly as possible into the shape of a ball on two stunted supports), strut about in circles, not all going the same way, but passing and crossing each other in various angles. As the " dance " proceeds the excitement of the birds increases, they stoop toward the ground, twist and turn, make sudden rushes forward stamping the ground with short quick beats of the feet, leaping over each other in their frenzy, then lowering their heads, exhaust the air in the sacs, producing a hollow sound that goes reverberating through the still air of the breaking day. Suddenly they become quiet, and walk about like creatures whose sanity is unquestioned, when some male again becomes possessed, and starts off on a rampage, and the " attack " from which he suffers becomes infectious and all the other birds at once give evidences of having taken the same disease, which then proceeds with a regular development to the usual conclusion. As the sun gets well above the horizon, and night's shadows have all been hurried away, the antics of the birds cease, the booming no longer resounds over the prairie, and the Grouse scatter in search of food, and in pursuit of their daily avocations. While this performance is always to be seen in the spring, it is not unusually indulged in for a brief turn in the autumn, and while it may be considered as essentially a custom of the breeding season, yet like the drumming of the Ruffed Grouse, it may be regarded also as an exhibition of the birds' vigor and vitality, indulged in at periods of the year even when the breeding season has long passed.

There seems to be no spot especially favored by the hen as a site for the nest, so long as it affords suitable concealment. With the shelter of some bush, along the bank of a stream where the cover is somewhat dense, or in the midst of a clump of weeds, in thickets on the hillside, or in a bunch of grass out on the open prairie, she is equally satisfied, and in a slight hollow arched over with grass deposits her eggs. These are precisely like those of the Columbian Sharp-tailed Grouse, and the usual number in a clutch is about a dozen, though sometimes considerably more are laid, and but one brood is raised in a season. The hen is a very close sitter, and her plumage harmonizes so well with her surroundings that it is a very difficult matter to discover her on the nest. In about three weeks the chicks appear, and the mother is very solicitous for their welfare, leading them in search of insects, which at first comprise their means of subsistence, and keeping them near some thickets where they can easily hide on the approach of danger. She clucks to them like a domestic hen, and shelters them under her wings from the storm. In spite of all her care many a downy chick disappears, borne away in the talons of some Hawk which has swooped suddenly upon the brood from an unlooked for quarter, or else a watchful fox or other quadruped, or gliding snake, has snatched one of the little creatures as it chased some flying insect. Not many of the members of a brood that is hatched reach maturity, for numerous vacancies from various causes are usually created in the ranks. Toward the last of September the young are about full grown, and at this time they lie well to the dog, and generally are not wild. The flock does not rise simultaneously, always some of its members remaining after the others are well upon the wing. As they flush they utter a cackling cry, and this is often repeated with each beat of the wings, even after they have flown for some distance. The flight is mostly performed in a straight line, except where the nature of the ground makes it an impossibility, and is swift, the bird being borne along by alternate flappings and sailings. When the wings are held motionless, they are much curved, with the primaries spread far apart toward the tips, and turned down. If many coveys occupy similar tracts of country they keep their little family parties separate and distinct from each other, and if they have not been much molested will permit one to approach very near them without exhibiting any signs of alarm. In the autumn, in such localities as the Bad Lands of the Dakotas, they are in the habit of passing much of their time in the "coulées" or wooded ravines, into which they always fly for shelter if by chance they have been flushed anywhere in the open grounds, or among the buttes. When scattered in these ravines excellent sport can be had with them, as they lie close and generally rise singly, and as the sportsman is frequently above them, they present easy marks as they fly out of the bushes into the open, or rise above the cover if declining to leave the place of refuge.

The Prairie Sharp-tail or White-belly, as it is sometimes called, is partly migratory, and, as I have already said, its habits vary somewhat in the different seasons, being a good deal of a prairie dweller in the summer, but more of a woodland bird in the winter. But this is natural, as it would not be likely to remain on the storm-swept plains during the severe weather, if the shelter that the trees afforded was near at hand and easily secured. In the autumn and winter the flocks unite and form great packs of several hundred individuals and are then wary and very watchful, running swiftly away from any object that alarms them, or taking wing when yet a long distance off. The flight is also much more protracted at this time, the packs frequently keeping on until lost to view.

At this period they are in the habit of perching much in trees, frequently on the tops of houses or any outlying buildings. I have often seen a tree nearly full of Grouse, so thickly were they assembled on the branches, some sitting close to the limbs looking more like great bunches without any particular shape at all, while others would stand upright in a stiff, constrained attitude, with the neck drawn out to its fullest extent and held motionless, and the legs showing to the full extent of the thighs. Sometimes they will remain in such situations even though shot at more than once, and occasionally a number may be killed, if the lowest in the tree is selected, so that the falling body may not alarm the living birds and cause them to take flight. They appear much magnified when on the branches, especially if their forms be sharply outlined against the sky. If much hunted their behavior in the trees changes, and as soon as anyone is seen approaching, the birds are at once on the *qui vive*, and, motionless, regard intently the object of their fears. Soon a warning *kluck* is heard, every head is raised and neck outstretched, and then with a loud *kluck* one bird takes wing, to be followed immediately by all the rest, uttering many *kluck-klucks* as they go. Usually they alight at no great distance, but their watchfulness is not lessened, and if pursued, the same tactics are repeated. The food of this Grouse consists of insects, leaves, berries, and, wherever it grows, the hips of the wild rose, whose hard seeds, answering the purpose of gravel in helping to grind the food, are greedily eaten. It also feeds on grain when readily accessible, for as a rule these birds do not

keep much about cultivated lands, and enter fields probably more for the insects they may be able to find there
than with the view of obtaining grain.   The flesh of the
Prairie Sharp-tail is like its congeners', light-colored when
the bird is young but dark in the adult, and if you are not
compelled by stress of circumstances to eat it three times
a day, as I have been, is very palatable.   It is a noble
bird, game in the fullest and truest sense of the word,
and presents a beautiful sight as it walks easily and gracefully over the prairie, raising at intervals its lengthened
crest, and looking back at its observer, with its clear
liquid eyes betokening a trust and confidence that is, alas!
too often misplaced.   The Sharp-tailed and the Pinnated
Grouse often meet on the limits of their dispersion, but
rarely mingle together, for they are deadly enemies and
engage in desperate battles; the habits and dispositions
of the birds causing them to lead different lives and seek
dissimilar habitats.   To my mind the Sharp-tail is the
finer and handsomer bird.

PEDIŒCETES PHASIANELLUS CAMPESTRIS.

Geographical Distribution.—Prairies east of Rocky Mountains from Montana to New Mexico, and from Wisconsin and
Illinois to Colorado.

Adult Male.—Entire upper parts, buff, ochraceous upon back
and scapulars, blotched and barred with black; scapulars
streaked with white, and large white spots on tips of wing-coverts; primaries, dark brown, spotted with white on outer webs;
spot in front of eye, sides of face and throat, light buff, with a
cluster of brown spots on the cheeks; under parts, white, with
lengthened V-shaped brown lines on each feather, most numerous on breast, where they are the predominant color; middle of
abdomen and under tail-coverts, white; central tail feathers extend beyond the rest, and are barred with black and ochraceous;
legs, brownish white; maxilla, black, mandible, horn color at

base, black at tip. Total length, about 16½ inches; wing, 8½; tail, 5¼.

Adult Female is slightly smaller than the male, and the central tail feathers are shorter. Otherwise resembles him in her plumage.

Downy Young.—Upper parts, buff, irregularly marked with lines and spots of black, broadest upon the back; wings, barred with white and black; under parts, lemon yellow, inclined to buff upon the breast; bill, light yellow; culmen, brown.

SAGE GROUSE.

LARGEST of all American Grouse, and only exceeded in size by the Cock of the Woods or Capercailzie of the Old World, the Sage Grouse is an inhabitant of the barren plains where the sage bush (Artemisia) grows, the leaves of which constitute its principal food. Its range is from Assiniboia and British Columbia in the north to New Mexico in the south, and from the Dakotas in the east to California, Oregon, and Washington in the west. It is a resident and breeds wherever found, and only makes a partial migration when the sage bushes become hidden beneath great falls of snow, compelling it to seek other localities with less elevation. The Cock of the Plains is rarely met with far from the localities covered by the sage bush, for the leaves of this plant appear to be a necessity for its existence. Although its crop may show that other food has been swallowed, yet the major portion of the contents will always be sage leaves, and these impart a very bitter and disagreeable taste to the flesh, if the bird is not drawn immediately after it is killed. Besides these leaves, this species feeds on insects, berries, wild pease, the pods and blossoms of various plants, and grain.

Its stomach is a soft and membranous bag, and it has, properly speaking, no gizzard. This would seem to indicate that the bird was not a grain feeder, but individuals have been killed whose stomachs were filled with wheat, showing that, in spite of a lack of grinding power, the bird is able to digest grain. Its diet, however, is chiefly

30. Sage Grouse.

leaves and the tender portions of plants. It is a hardy bird, bearing the extremes of heat and cold apparently without inconvenience, and I have seen it walking leisurely about under the rays of a torrid sun, or exposed to the fierce, keen blasts of a December storm that would make most creatures seek the nearest shelter.

During the blizzards and other heavy storms that so frequently sweep over the country it inhabits, the Sage Cock takes refuge amid the dense clumps of the sage bushes, or in the " coulées " or small valleys that intersect the plains at intervals, where it obtains sufficient protection from the blasts. Although this species is so large, its plumage harmonizes so well with the bird's surroundings that it is at times exceedingly difficult to see it, and it is not an unusual occurrence to pass within a few feet of one or more Sage Grouse, without noticing them at all, if they remain motionless, as they generally do. Early in March the pairing season begins, and the male commences to court the females. His actions at this time are not unlike those of the Pinnated and Sharp-tailed Grouse already described, but the air sacs on each side of the neck, when inflated, are so enormous that the bird appears much more grotesque than the males of the other species. These air bladders extend both forward and upward, and his head practically disappears between them, making his neck seem altogether too top-heavy for him to preserve his balance. The long pointed feathers of the tail are spread out to the fullest extent, the wings trail along the ground, and the spiny feathers along the air sacs stand straight out. In this ludicrous attitude, which no doubt the bird considers as the very acme of perfect beauty and attractiveness, he struts before the admiring gaze of the assembled hens, uttering subdued guttural sounds. This exhibition having accomplished its legitimate purpose, a suitable place is selected for the nest, generally under some sage bush. The receptacle for the eggs is a very primitive affair, a slight hollow, sparsely lined with grass and a few feathers; or sometimes the eggs are dropped upon the bare ground. These are quite large, olive-buff in color, tinged with green, covered with dots and spots of chocolate brown, and vary considerably from each other, some being of a pale green tint with sharply defined spots of chocolate, others a pale buff without any tinge of green, thickly covered with fine chocolate dots, or spotted and dotted with the same. These markings are all superficial and can be easily wiped off, leaving the egg a uniform greenish white. The number usually found in a nest varies from seven to seventeen, the latter, however, being quite unusual. Ten would seem to be about a fair average.

About three weeks is the period of incubation, and the hen is a very close sitter, and will seldom leave her nest until almost trodden upon, which occurrence is very likely to happen, as it is such a difficult matter to distinguish her from the objects around. While the hen is sitting, and also when she is rearing the young, the male takes no share in her duties, nor troubles himself in any way with her cares and anxieties, but amuses himself in the company of other cocks as neglectful of their wives as himself, and they do not join the coveys until the young have attained their full growth. When half grown the flesh of the Sage Hen is very tender and palatable, but even then the bird must be drawn as soon as killed. It is not always easy to flush these birds, as they will run long distances before taking wing, and skulk and hide at every opportunity. But when forced to rise, they flush with a great fluttering of the wings and utter a loud *kck-kck-kck*, which kind of cackle is kept up for quite a considerable time. They seem to have difficulty in getting well on the wing, and rise heavily, wabbling from side to side as if trying to gain an equilibrium, but once started they go far and fast enough, with intermittent quick beats of the pinions and easy sailing on motionless wings.

As a rule the Sage Grouse is not very wild, and a covey, when anyone draws near, will at first walk quietly along, frequently within easy gunshot, and it is not until they are persistently followed, or one suddenly dashes into a covey, that they take wing. It requires a hard blow to bring them down, and large shot are necessary to kill them, for they are capable, even if severely wounded, of carrying away large quantities of lead, and will fly a long distance, probably not stopping until life is extinct. The number in a covey is usually small, much less than is observed in many other species of Grouse, ranging, according to my observation, from seven to ten, often not over five or six. These are probably the survivors of the original brood which has been decimated by adverse weather, such as heavy storms and wet seasons, during which many chicks succumb to the onslaught of various enemies both furred and feathered, not to mention man, the most destructive enemy of all.

In the winter the coveys gather together in great packs; sometimes a hundred birds are assembled in one immense flock, and great is the commotion and loud the whirring and beating of wings and vociferous cackling when from any cause they rise in the air. The members of a family roost in a circle on the ground, in the manner described in the article on Bob White, so that in case of alarm each great bird has a fair way of escape directly in front of him, without danger of being impeded or incommoded by his neighbor as he rises from the ground. It never perches or settles in trees, but sometimes is seen mounted on a branch of a sage bush, a few feet from the ground. It keeps away from the woods, and is, as its name implies, a bird of the plains, a familiar feature of those vast, desert, treeless districts, covered by the peculiar pale green sage bush. The Sage Grouse may be able to go a long time without water, but if it is readily obtained, as when they are in the vicinity of a spring or small stream, they are accustomed to drink twice a day, in the early morning, and again at evening. Sometimes considerable numbers are gathered together at such places, especially if the localities which contain a supply of water are widely separated. Like the Pinnated and Sharp-tailed Grouse, members of flocks of the present species do not all flush together, but always one or more remain after the main body is on the wing; and when hunting them, it is not well to take it for granted that all have departed until the ground in the vicinity has been well searched, for it is pretty certain that at least one bird will be found which had vainly considered itself securely hidden and safe from discovery. The Sage Grouse is a large and heavy bird, the males frequently measuring two and a half feet in length, and weighing at times as much as eight pounds. The female is considerably smaller, so much so that occasionally the discrepancy is so great as to cause remark; but as may be supposed in such large birds, the individuals of neither sex are always of the same size, and those of lesser growth can find, if needed, mates not disproportionate to themselves. It is a splendid bird, which any country may be proud to claim as native to its boundaries, and may it long be preserved to enliven the desolate regions among which it dwells!

CENTROCERCUS UROPHASIANUS.

Geographical Distribution.—British Columbia and Assiniboia in the north to New Mexico, Utah, and Nevada. East to the Dakotas, Nebraska, and Colorado, and west to California, Oregon, and Washington.

Adult Male.—Upper parts, light brown or grayish, barred with black, dark brown, and grayish, sometimes blotched with black; wings, like the back, with borders of tertials, and central streaks and bars of some of the coverts, white; primaries, grayish brown, lighter on their outer webs; tail, composed of twenty cuneate feathers, graduated to a filamentous point, the central ones like the back, remainder black, barred with light buff for two-thirds their length from the base; top of head and neck, grayish buff, barred with black, chin, throat, and cheeks, white, spotted on first with black, sometimes this part is all black; a blackish line from mouth passes under the eye, and over the ear-coverts; a white line extends from behind the eye down side of neck; fore-neck, black, bordered with grayish white; chest, gray, with the shafts of feathers very stiff and black; flanks, barred broadly with blackish brown and buffy white, occasionally a buff line in center of black bar, sometimes mottled with black; abdomen and rest of lower parts, jet-black; under tail-coverts, black, broadly tipped with white; bill, black. Total length, about 28 inches; wing, 13; tail, 13. Weight, 5 to 8 pounds.

On sides of neck is a loose skin which, in the breeding season, is inflated into two enormous yellow sacs, and by the exhaustion of the air a loud, booming sound is produced.

Adult Female.—Like the male, but much smaller, the chin and throat, pure white. Total length, about 22 inches; wing, 10½; tail, 8¼.

Downy Young.—Upper parts, grayish brown, irregularly marked and blotched with black, most conspicuous on the head. Markings of lower parts indistinctly defined.

WILLOW PTARMIGAN.

IN the northern portions of the Northern Hemisphere, dwelling amid the snow and desolate places, the Willow Grouse ranges throughout the Arctic regions of the globe, and is found around the world in the high latitudes. In the New World it is a resident of the fur countries, and dwells from the Arctic Ocean to Sitka and the Chilcat Peninsula on the Pacific Coast, and across the Continent, in the east, coming down in winter to northern New York. In the latter season it is very abundant in different portions of Canada. In the spring the Ptarmigan descends to the low grounds and the male begins his singular maneuvers to entice some female to join him. Selecting some particular spot, generally a slight elevation, he struts about with lowered wings and expanded tail, head thrown back, and the red combs over the eyes erect and conspicuous, takes a short flight upward, and then sails around in a circle, descending slowly on curved wings, alighting usually at or near the place from which he arose, uttering all the time short quick notes resembling a petulant, hoarse bark. Regaining his first position he calls in a different note several times repeated, and in a few moments again makes his circular flight.

If the birds are numerous in the locality many males will be seen executing similar movements, and the air resounds with their barking notes. In due course the females appear in the vicinity, and then the males are excited to frenzy and desperate battles occur among them,

31. Willow Ptarmigan.

carried on with great energy and undaunted resolution, the feathers flying in all directions. The birds at this period are usually in the transition plumage from winter to summer, some red feathers having already begun to appear on the neck, but the regular moult is not really completely finished until several weeks later. By the middle of May the birds have about all succeeded in obtaining mates, and the nesting season begins. A shallow depression in the ground is lined loosely with dried leaves and grass, and on an average eight or nine eggs are deposited; sometimes as many as thirteen and even seventeen have been found in one nest. They differ greatly in detail, though having a general resemblance. The shape varies from an ovate to an elongate ovate, and the ground color from cream to reddish buff, frequently hidden by a mass of dark reddish, blackish brown, or black blotches and vermiculations, which cover nearly all the shell. Sometimes these are small and mingled together in a confused mass, and again they are distributed in patches, groups, or singly with some indications of form, very irregular though it may be, and no two eggs are exactly alike. Occasionally if, after the complement of eggs has been laid, they are all removed, the hen will deposit another set of about, if not quite, the same number.

The period of incubation is about seventeen days, and the chicks follow the parents as soon as hatched. Only one brood is raised in a season. Unlike the majority of the members of the Grouse family, the male Ptarmigan remains constantly in the vicinity of the nest while the female is sitting, and expresses the strongest disapprobation of which he is capable at any interference with the process of incubation, and especially if an attempt is made to carry away the eggs, uttering his hoarse call in angry remonstrance. Both parents are very devoted to, and solicitous for, their young, and will permit anyone to come very near, indeed almost touch them, when they are accompanied by their chicks. The hen sits very close during incubation, leaving the nest only for short intervals, and so unwilling is she to desert her treasures that she will permit herself almost to be trodden upon, and frequently she has allowed herself to be captured by hand rather than secure her own safety by flight. Before incubation is finished, she becomes quite denuded of feathers on the abdomen. The young are pretty creatures, very captivating, as are all chicks, and have a downy dress of greenish buff or sulphur yellow, decorated with chestnut and black. When they are half grown they begin to fly, but do not attain their full size until late in the autumn.

Ptarmigan, as it appears to me, are in a constant state of moult; and I have rarely seen a specimen that did not have pin-feathers on some part of its body, no matter at what period of the year it was killed. The assumption of the summer plumage commences on the neck, where a few colored feathers appear, and the birds, during the transition from the pure white winter garb to the bright summer dress, present a curious piebald and mottled appearance. They do not all moult at the same time, some assuming the complete nuptial dress considerably before the rest, and it is difficult to determine whether one sex is in advance of the other in moulting, and if so, which one it is. The cold rains and damp heavy fogs and mists, so prevalent in the regions frequented by these birds, cause the death of numbers of the young, to whom a complete wetting is usually fatal, and many also perish at the loss of the old birds, which have met their fate either by gun or snare, when the little creatures were too small to take care of themselves. The Indians destroy a great many, for chicken Grouse, even if still in the egg, is considered a great delicacy by them.

During the winter Ptarmigan feed on the small twigs of the willow and various bushes, and as the snow disappears, on any berries that may have remained from the last autumn, frozen though they may be, and later, on insects of various kinds. In the spring the birds make a partial migration, coming from the shelter of the valleys and forests, where they have passed the winter, into the open country when the bare spots left by the vanishing snow begin to appear. In the autumn also they seek the shelter of the woods and travel to the southward, and when the snow has covered the landscape these birds, when migrating, assemble in great flocks, sometimes amounting to many thousands, and the noise of their myriad wings, as the great host rises from the ground, makes, as it has been expressed, "both the air and earth to tremble." When young the flesh of the Ptarmigan is white and delicate, but that of the adult is dark and of little flavor, save when the bird has been feeding on the buds of the willow, when it is rather bitter.

Immense numbers are taken in snares by the Esquimaux and Indians of the frozen North; one man frequently, in a single day, capturing a sledge-load. This great slaughter is accomplished while the birds are migrating to or from their summer resorts. A number of bushes is set out across the line of their march and the branches filled with nooses of sinew, and the birds come in such great numbers that they are captured in thousands, entering the snares so fast that a man cannot kill and release them quickly enough. Another method is to take advantage of the pugnacity and amorous feeling of the male during the breeding season. A native takes a stuffed skin of a cock and secure it to a stick thrust in the body. He then seeks a spot where a pair are busily occupied with their marital duties, and, fastening a small net, which he carries with him, to the ground, places the decoy bird near it. In a few moments the live male sees it and comes immediately forward ready for a fight, frequently seizing the counterfeit and pulling and tugging at it with great determination. While so engaged the net is dropped over him, and his warfare is soon finished.

Like the Ruffed Grouse and other members of the family, the Ptarmigan frequently passes the night under the snow, diving into it head first, and emerging again in the morning with a sudden leap into the air. Neither when entering or leaving the snow is a foot ever put upon it, and this precaution is doubtless to prevent the discovery of the bird's hiding place by any quadruped who might otherwise be able to track it by following the scent left by the feet, and pounce upon it in its sleeping quarters. Doubtless many perish in such places by a crust forming during the night, when the birds would be imprisoned, but probably, in the high latitudes in which Ptarmigan usually dwell, thaws are very infrequent and the danger from that source much lessened. The change from the summer dress to the pure white one of winter takes place in the autumn, and is effected much more rapidly than is the assumption of the summer plumage. The feathers change on the abdomen first and on the back and head last, the reverse of the spring moult. In the far North this bird, together with the caribou, constitutes the most important food supply of the natives of those bleak regions, without which they would frequently be in danger of starvation; but the birds abound in such numbers, and they are naturally so fear-

32. Willow Ptarmigan in Winter.

less and tame, rarely making any very serious effort
to escape from man (even in more southern localities,
where they are much hunted), that it is not a very difficult matter, even without firearms, to secure at one time
enough to satisfy the members of a moderately large
community.

LAGOPUS LAGOPUS.

Geographical Distribution.—Arctic regions of both Hemispheres. In America ranging south to Sitka and British Provinces, Newfoundland, accidental in New England.

Adult Male in Summer Plumage.—Top of head, back of neck,
and entire upper parts, barred with chestnut, ochraceous, and
black, some feathers having their central portions all black, forming blotches, and more or less of the feathers tipped with grayish
white; scapulars and tertials like the back; primaries, white, with
dark brown shafts; secondaries, white, with white shafts; in some
specimens the shafts of the primaries are nearly black, and the
coloring extends over a portion of the inner web; throat, sides of
neck, and breast, light chestnut, darkest on lower part of breast,
barred everywhere except on throat with black; flanks, dark
brown, barred and mottled with black, occasionally a buff bar
appearing among the black ones; entire rest of under parts, with
legs and toes, pure white; upper tail-coverts, like the back; tail,
black, extreme base and tip, white; bill, black. Total length,
about 14 inches; wing, 7¾; tail, 5½.

Some examples have the sides of head, throat, fore-neck, and
upper parts of breast uniform chestnut, becoming darker at
times, indeed almost black toward the white under parts.

Adult Female in Summer Plumage.—Top of head, back of
neck, and entire upper parts, with upper tail-coverts, black, barred
with ochraceous, and feathers tipped with white; scapulars, tertials, and some of the wing-coverts, like the back ; throat, sides
and front of neck, buff, with an ochraceous tinge on cheeks,
barred irregularly with black, the bars taking more the form of
spots on the throat; entire rest of under parts and under tail-
coverts, buff, coarsely barred with black, some feathers having
nearly white tips; primaries and secondaries, white, the former
with dark brown shafts; tail, brownish black, tipped with white,

and base also white; legs and toes covered with brownish white feathers; bill, black. Total length, about 14 inches; wing, 7¾; tail, 5¼.

Downy Young.—General color of body, olive-buff, tinged with ochraceous on breast, back, and wings; throat and under parts lightest; top of head and occiput, chestnut, bordered with black; spot on lores, ear-coverts, line down hind-neck and broader lines on back, black.

Winter Plumage.—Entire body, pure white; tail, black, tipped with white.

ALLEN'S PTARMIGAN.

THIS bird, which is an inhabitant of Newfoundland, has been separated from the Willow Grouse as a sub-species on what must be considered as very slight and in-sufficient grounds. It is a very common species in the island, frequenting similar localities as does the Willow Grouse on the continent of America, and in its economy and habits in no way differs from that species. It is called Partridge by some, and feeds on seeds and buds and leaves of various trees and bushes; and great num-bers of them are killed annually. It bears a very close resemblance to the Willow Grouse, and requires more than an expert to discover wherein it differs; the chief and about the only perceptible distinction claimed is that the shafts of the secondaries and primaries are black in-stead of white. The description given of the habits of the Willow Grouse in the previous article will, in nearly all particulars, answer perfectly well for the present bird.

From the specimens which I have examined at various times during the past thirty years I fail to find any which present characters that would enable the Newfoundland bird to be distinguished from the Willow Grouse of other localities. The describer of Allen's Ptarmigan estab-lished the race upon the "shafts of both primaries and secondaries black, and by having the wing feathers, even some of the coverts marked and mottled with blackish." These characters do not seem to be reliable, and there are at present before me two males belonging to the collection of the American Museum of Natural History,

New York, numbered 26,857 and 26,858 respectively, from Humbert River, Newfoundland, collected by L. A. Zerega on September 15, 1886, which are so like the Fort Chimo bird described under *Lagopus lagopus* that the description there given will answer perfectly well for them. The shafts of the secondaries in both are pure white, and the shafts of primaries are a blackish brown, this color extending a little upon the webs near the tips. The color of the upper parts is almost identically the same, but one of the Newfoundland birds has more feathers tipped with grayish white, which is to be expected, as the specimen was killed five days later in the year than the Fort Chimo bird. If there is a distinct race of the Willow Grouse in Newfoundland, then the specific form is also found there, and it is very unlikely that birds from the same island, so closely allied, would maintain recognizable characters sufficient to separate them, when it is notorious that individuals even of the same flock vary so greatly from each other, both in color and markings, that it is practically impossible to procure two exactly alike at any season of the year. When writing my monograph of the Tetraoninæ I had a number of Newfoundland birds sent to me by the late Professor Baird, and I was unable then to discover any character sufficient to separate them from other Willow Grouse, and before we can accept a new race from that island as an established fact I think other and better characters than any yet known will have to be established.

33. Rock Ptarmigan.

ROCK PTARMIGAN.

ALONG the Alaskan coast, from the peninsula and Behring Sea, throughout the mountains of the interior, and across the Arctic regions of North America to Hudson Bay, southern Labrador, and the island of Greenland, the Rock Ptarmigan is a constant resident; frequenting low hills, or higher ranges in the summer, going down to the valleys during winter for shelter from the severity of the Northern climate at that season. It is also found on the Barren Grounds (the height of land lying between the Anderson and Wilmot Horton or Mac-Farlane rivers and thence inward to the western sea-bank of Franklin Bay), but is not so plentiful there as the Willow Grouse. It is more a bird of the mountains, and prefers to remain on elevated summits throughout the summer and amid precipitous slopes and rugged cliffs. It is a smaller bird than the Willow Grouse, and can always be distinguished from it by the black stripe running from the bill to the eye, which is present in both the summer and winter dress of the males.

In Alaska nesting begins in April, but in the eastern part of the birds' range not until the middle of June, sometimes even later. The nest resembles that of the Willow Ptarmigan, but the number of eggs is less, about seven, though occasionally many more are found in one nest—whether the product of one hen or not it would be difficult to say, but the probabilities are in favor of such a supposition, as I am not aware of any instance where two hens have been observed to occupy the same nest.

The eggs are hardly distinguishable from those of the Willow Grouse, but are smaller, and the markings rather less inclined to run into blotches, and possibly more distinct on that account. The female, like the Willow Ptarmigan, sits very closely on her nest, and it is very difficult to discover her, even when she is in an exposed position. During the mating season the male goes through similar antics to the Willow Grouse, uttering harsh, guttural notes in the air and descending on stiffened wings. At this time the combs over the eyes become a brilliant orange red, and at each end is a filamentous fringe, very conspicuous. He struts also in a similar manner to his relative, with spread tail and trailing wings, the neck frequently outstretched and lowered, and uttering at the same time a curious croak.

This species does not collect in large flocks, small parties usually going together as if they were only the members of one family, which is probably the case, and there is less pugnacity exhibited than is witnessed among the Willow Grouse. The change of plumage from winter to summer and *vice versa* takes place about the same time as in the other species, and these birds always seem to have pin-feathers amid their plumage, as if the perfect costume had never at any time been quite attained, and this, I believe, is the fact among the majority of individuals, for even when one part of the body is in full dress other portions are in a transition state, and when these last are perfected, the first have already begun to change. And if a bird succeeds in arranging himself entirely in a full suit, he must be able to wear it but for a very brief period. The habits of this species are very similar to the Willow Grouse.

34. Rock Ptarmigan in Winter.

LAGOPUS RUPESTRIS.

Geographical Distribution.—Arctic America, Alaska to Labrador, south to Gulf of St. Lawrence, Greenland.

Adult Male in Summer.—Head, neck, and upper parts, gray, barred with black, and irregular rusty bars on the head, back of neck, upper back and scapulars, and black blotches on upper part of back; wings, like the back; primaries and outer secondaries, white, with brownish black shafts on the primaries; upper tail-coverts, gray, barred with black, and occasionally rusty, some feathers with white tips; tail, blackish brown, lighter on margins; breast, dark brown, feathers barred with white and black; entire rest of under parts and legs, pure white; lores, black; bill, black. Total length, 14 inches; wing, 7½; tail, 4½. Specimen from Labrador.

Adult Female in Summer.—Shot July 31. Head, entire upper parts, and wings, black, irregularly barred with white and deep buff, feathers generally tipped with white, broadest on upper tail-coverts, many of which have their outer margins deep buff; tail, smoky-brown, tipped with white; throat, breast, and flanks, ochraceous, barred with black, some white feathers showing; middle of abdomen, white; crissum and under tail-coverts, ochraceous, barred with black; feathers on thighs and legs, white; primaries, white, with pale brown shafts; secondaries and most of the wing-coverts, also white; bill, black. Total length, about 13 inches; wing, 7; tail, 4½. Specimen from Quickiock Falls, Labrador.

REINHARDT'S PTARMIGAN.

NORTHERN Labrador, the islands on the west of the Cumberland Gulf, Greenland, and both shores down to Hudson Strait, include the range of this Ptarmigan. It is common in Greenland and in the more elevated portions of Labrador. It appears to be a bird of the open and barren country, differing in this respect from the other species just preceding, which pass much of the year in wooded districts. The coveys scatter in May, when nesting and courting begin. Mr. Turner, who has had excellent opportunities for observing this bird in Labrador, says that at this period the male does not spring into the air like the Willow Grouse, but, with spreading tail and dragging wings, runs around the object of his affections, or else, with his breast pressed against the ground and outstretched neck, he strives to push himself along with his feet. At such times his feathers are all ruffled, his combs swollen and erect, and, while executing the most astonishing antics, such as tossing himself in the air unsupported by his wings, and even rolling over and over, as if quite crazy, he continues to utter a peculiar, growling *kurr-kurr*-like sound. The males are very pugnacious and fight desperately, and keep it up until one is completely exhausted, while the feathers that cover the ground attest the fierceness of the struggle. The hen seems quite indifferent as to the result of these conflicts, and shows little of the affection toward the male which he exhibits for her. The young are very delicate when first hatched, and doubtless many

35. Reinhardt's Ptarmigan.

perish in the sudden squalls of that changeable climate. They utter a soft *pe-pe-pe*, and are at first indistinguishable from the young of the Willow Grouse.

The food of this bird is the usual variety of seeds, insects, leaves, berries, and buds of different plants and trees, and one individual had his crop filled with sphagnum moss. They go in small coveys, and but one brood is raised in a season; each covey being composed, probably, of members of the same brood. The eggs, deposited in June in a nest similar to that of the Rock Ptarmigan, are absolutely indistinguishable from those of that species.

LAGOPUS RUPESTRIS REINHARDTI.

Geographical Distribution.—Northern Labrador, and islands on the west shore of Cumberland Gulf, Greenland.

Adult Male in Summer.—Very similar in general pattern of markings, and in coloration to *L. rupestris,* but not so regularly barred above, and the bars much coarser.

Adult Female in Summer.—Nautilik, Cumberland Gulf.—In general appearance this is a black and white bird, with the black predominating; top of head, back, rump, and upper tail-coverts, black, with from one to three buffy white spots on the outer edge of the webs, and each feather more or less distinctly tipped with white; a few feathers, mottled with pale buff and white for about one-third their length from the tip, are scattered over the back, these probably belonging to the plumage characteristic of autumn, and which will next be assumed; the throat, sides of head, and neck all around are buffy white, barred narrowly with black; scapulars, most of the secondaries, and greater wing-coverts are colored like the back, but all the feathers are tipped with white, giving this part a black and white appearance, with only occasionally pale buff spots showing; feathers of under parts, flanks, and under tail-coverts, barred with black and light buff, and tipped with white, but the black predominates; the flank feathers have much broader bars of both black and pale buff, and the latter is more conspicuous here than on any other part of the bird; tail, seal brown, edged with white at the tips;

legs, white; bill, dark horn color, lightest at tip; claws, horn color. Total length, $11\frac{7}{10}$ inches; wing, 7; tail, $4\frac{3}{10}$; tarsus, $1\frac{2}{10}$. Exposed culmen, half inch.

A Greenland specimen from Sukkertoppen, also an adult female, varies from the above described bird, in having more buff on the under parts, and considerable white on the abdomen; the flank feathers are also more buff, as the bars are decidedly buff. The date of capture of this example is not given and it is impossible to tell whether it has quite assumed the breeding plumage, or is passing from it, but as there are no feathers of an autumn dress visible it is probable that the breeding dress is not yet completed; the autumn dress seems to be ochraceous, mottled with black, and black blotches interspersed on the upper parts,

36. Welch's Ptarmigan.

WELCH'S PTARMIGAN.

THIS may be called the Rock Ptarmigan of Newfoundland, and is a dark-grayish bird with a bluish
tinge to the plumage, which has been likened to the
color of the Sooty Grouse, and all the feathers are dotted
with blackish. It is very numerous in the rocky portions
of the island it inhabits, distributed among the mountains in the interior, and is rather local, not going far
from the place in which it was reared. It may be considered the Alpine species of Newfoundland Ptarmigan,
not often met with below the line of spruce forest, except
when it descends in winter to feed on the buds of various
trees growing in the lowlands. It is sometimes called
the Mountain Partridge, and occasionally associates with
the Willow Grouse. Very little is known of its habits.

LAGOPUS RUPESTRIS WELCHI.

Geographical Distribution.—Mountains of Newfoundland.

Adult Male in Summer.—Entire upper parts, and upper
tail-coverts, brownish gray, vermiculated and spotted with
black, many feathers having white tips, and some with white
bars near the tips; front, chin, upper part of throat, cheeks,
and back of neck, barred with black and white; top of head,
rufous, blotched with black; lores, black; tail, blackish brown,
lighter toward the edges of the webs; a number of feathers barred
with black and white on upper part of breast; on lower breast,
belly, and under tail-coverts, white, interspersed on the first
with numerous feathers colored like the breast ; thighs and
feathers of tarsi, white; on toes, yellowish white; wing-coverts,
like the back; bill and claws, horn color. Total length, 14 inches;
wing, 7½; tail, 4½; tarsus, 1½; exposed culmen, ½ inch.

Adult Female in Summer.—The female in her summer dress is a very different bird, and has the top of the head broadly barred with black and deep yellow or buff; back and sides of neck and head, yellowish white, barred or spotted with black; entire upper parts, including upper tail-coverts, vermiculated with black and deep buff (some feathers almost black), edged and tipped with buff or white, this being particularly the case upon the upper part of back near the neck; wings, like the back, but primaries and secondaries white, the shafts of former, brown; tail, dark brown, the feathers with white bases and white edges to the tips ; four median feathers, black, irregularly barred with white, and tipped with white ; throat, yellowish white, becoming pale buff on the breast, the latter broadly barred in waving lines, with black ; flanks, also buff, with broad brownish black bars ; lower breast, abdomen, and under tail-coverts, buffy white, with occasional black bars visible; thighs, white; feathers of legs and feet, yellowish white; bill and claws, pale horn color.   Total length, about 12¼ inches; wing, 6⅔; tail, 4⅜; bill at gape, ¾; tarsus, 1⅜.

Adult Female in Autumn resembles the summer plumage of the male, but has a generally more grayish appearance, and with the back more conspicuously and profusely blotched with black; no indication of black upon the lores, but upon the flanks are occasional feathers broadly barred with black and white, the latter sometimes tinged with yellow, as is characteristic of the summer dress of the adult female; the throat and neck are more conspicuously barred with black and white than in the male, and have more the appearance of a white ground barred with black; the abdomen and under tail-coverts are pure white, and the tail feathers are tipped with white.

Winter Plumage, pure white, with a black loral streak in the male.

Edwin Sheppard.

37. Nelson's Ptarmigan.

NELSON'S PTARMIGAN.

THIS is a little-known race of Ptarmigan, specimens of which were procured by Mr. Nelson on Unalaska, one of the Aleutian Islands. It is said by Mr. Turner to be very abundant there, and also in Uminak, Akutan, and Akun, other islands of the same chain, and is a resident wherever found, seldom leaving the island in which it was born. It prefers rocky ledges, but roosts and rears its young in the valleys. The mating season commences in May and lasts about three weeks, and the nest is usually placed in the tall grass. It is a very careless affair, composed of a little grass and some feathers from the hen's breast, and before incubation is completed the eggs are generally lying on the bare ground. The number of these varies from nine to seventeen, but eleven is the usual number. The period of incubation was not ascertained. The birds never go in large flocks, those that were seen being apparently the parents and their brood of a previous year.

LAGOPUS RUPESTRIS NELSONI.

Geographical Distribution.—Islands of Unalaska, Unimak, Akutan, and Akun. Aleutian Chain.

Adult Male in Summer.—General color of entire plumage, dark russet, finely vermiculated with black, the center of the feathers showing occasionally as blotches; feathers of head and neck, tipped with ochraceous, giving this part a lighter hue than the rest; lores and space beneath the eyes, black; comb over eye, scarlet; throat, white, barred with black; jugulum, breast, and flanks, much lighter than the back, vermiculated with black, and with occasionally apical black bars and white tips; inner secondaries and tertials, like the back; wing-coverts generally, and many of the secondaries and primaries, white, the latter with brownish shafts; abdomen and rest of under parts, white, the former mottled with black; under tail-coverts, white; thighs, white; bill, black; claws, dark horn color. Total length, $13\frac{3}{16}$ inches; wing, $7\frac{3}{8}$; tail, $4\frac{3}{8}$; tarsus, $1\frac{3}{8}$; bill, 1; exposed culmen, $\frac{3}{4}$.

Adult Female in Spring.—Head and upper parts, tawny ochraceous, almost tawny, barred with black, and most of the feathers tipped with white; tertials and innermost secondaries, similarly marked and colored, but with not so bright a hue; secondaries, most of wing-coverts, and primaries, white, with pale brown shafts; middle tail feathers, like the back, remainder, clove brown, with white bases and tips; chin, white; throat, breast, and flanks, bright ochraceous, barred with black, and many feathers with white tips; center of breast and belly, white; under tail-coverts, pale ochraceous, barred regularly with black; thighs and tarsi, white; bill and claws, black. Total length, $13\frac{1}{4}$ inches; wing, $7\frac{3}{8}$; tail, $4\frac{1}{2}$; tarsus, 1; bill, $\frac{3}{4}$; exposed culmen, $\frac{1}{2}$ inch.

The females of this subspecies vary in color, some being very much lighter than the one just described, with correspondingly broader black and white markings, and the white much clearer and purer.

The Winter Plumage is pure white in both sexes, but the male has a black loral streak.

38. Turner's Ptarmigan.

TURNER'S PTARMIGAN.

AN inhabitant of the western part of the Aleutian chain, this bird is quite numerous on Atka, Amchitka, and Attu islands. It was discovered by Mr. Turner, who has furnished all that is known about it. He says that he was struck with its great size, shape of the bill, and length of claws, and it frequents the lowlands and hills of the western islands, and builds its nest among the rank grasses near the beach. This is carelessly made of dried grass and similar materials, and the eggs, varying in number from eleven to seventeen, are darker in color than those of the Rock Ptarmigan, and slightly smaller than those of the Willow Grouse. In habits it resembles the first species. On account of the number of foxes on Attu this bird frequents higher elevations than it is accustomed to do on the other islands. The natives assert that this Ptarmigan is also found on Agattu and, on account of the absence of foxes, is quite numerous on that island.

LAGOPUS RUPESTRIS ATKENSIS.

Geographical Distribution.—Islands of Atka, Amchitka, Attu and possibly Agattu of the Aleutian Chain.

Adult Male in Summer.—Head and neck, tawny ochraceous, barred with black, rest of upper parts, dark russet on basal two-thirds of feathers, remainder gray, very finely vermiculated and dotted with black; some small black spots upon the scapulars, but there is a general absence of the black spots upon the back, so conspicuous in *L. r. townsendi;* upper tail-coverts, like the . back; tail, clove brown, feathers tipped with white widest on the central feathers; greater wing-coverts, scapulars, and innermost secondaries like the back; rest of wing, pure white, with black shafts to the primaries; the throat is white, sides of face and breast, like the head and neck, but the breast and flanks are more finely barred and vermiculated, while scattered about the sides of head and along the flanks are many white feathers; rest of under parts, thighs, and tarsi, pure white; loral space, black; a crimson or scarlet comb over the eye; bill, black; claws, horn color, with white tips. Total length, $13\frac{5}{8}$ inches; wing, $7\frac{3}{8}$; tail, $4\frac{5}{8}$; tarsus, $1\frac{5}{16}$; exposed culmen, $\frac{5}{8}$.

It is possible that this specimen is not in what may be called perfect summer plumage, as the throat is white. This part would undoubtedly, for a few days at least, be colored like the neck, but the plumage of these birds varies so from day to day that it is only by accident that one is procured in what may be termed the full and perfect summer dress.

Female in Summer.—Head and entire upper parts, and most of the wing, ochraceous, barred with black, the bars narrower and more numerous on lower back and upper tail-coverts, with most of the feathers tipped with white; primaries and secondaries, white, the former with blackish brown shafts; throat, neck, breast, flanks, and under parts, generally including under tail-coverts, ochraceous, barred irregularly and narrowly with black ; tail, clove-brown, with outer web finely mottled with buff for two-thirds the basal length of central feathers, and growing gradually less on the lateral ones ; bill, black ; claws, black, with white tips. Total length, $13\frac{1}{2}$ inches; wing, $7\frac{3}{8}$; tail, $4\frac{8}{8}$; tarsus, $1\frac{3}{4}$.

Winter Plumage is pure white, with black loral streak in the male.

39. Townsend's Ptarmigan.

TOWNSEND'S PTARMIGAN.

THIS is another species of Ptarmigan that has been seen by few naturalists in its wild state, and was brought from the Aleutian islands of Kyska and Adak by Mr. Townsend, after whom it has been named. Only about twenty specimens were procured, and the visitors' sojourn at the islands was too brief for any particular knowledge of the birds' habits to be gained.

Probably, like other of its relatives in the Aleutian chain, it will never become an object for the sportsman's pursuit, the island on which it lives being situated too far away from all civilization to be easily accessible.

LAGOPUS RUPESTRIS TOWNSENDI.

Geographical Distribution.—Kyska and Adak Islands, Aleutian Chain.

Adult Male in Summer.—General color of entire upper parts, including head and neck, together with the breast and flanks, raw umber, with a tinge of russet, finely vermiculated with black on lower back and rump, more coarsely marked on the other parts with black blotches on the head, neck, upper part of back and wings; feathers of back, rump, and wings tipped with white; some of these white tips are finely spotted with black, giving to them a gray appearance; the outer secondaries, tertials, and most of the wing-coverts and primaries, pure white, the last having black shafts; the long upper tail-coverts are marked and colored like the back, with white tips; tail, clove-brown, nearly black, the feathers tipped with white, broadest on the middle pair, and decreasing on the outer ones, where it is either hardly perceptible or absent altogether; throat, white, mixed with a few colored feathers; breast, sides of neck, and flanks, ochraceous, barred with black, the bars broader and more conspicuous on neck; abdomen and belly, white; under tail-coverts, mummy brown, barred with black; loral space and ring around the eye, black, and a scarlet comb above the eye; side of neck, of a slightly paler hue than back or breast. Total length, $13\frac{1}{16}$ inches; wing, $7\frac{1}{2}$; tail, 4; tarsus, $1\frac{1}{2}$; exposed culmen, $\frac{1}{2}$.

Adult Female in Summer.—Entire upper parts, including scapulars, tertials, and upper tail-coverts, ochraceous, blotched and barred with black, most of the feathers tipped with white, except those on hind-neck, which are tipped with ochraceous; tail, square, clove-brown, the four median feathers tipped with white; secondaries, wing-coverts, and primaries, white, with black shafts, except those of inner secondaries, which are white; throat, white; breast, sides of body, and under tail-coverts, ochraceous buff, lighter than the back, and broadly barred with black; center of breast, abdomen, and belly, pure white; thighs and tarsus covered with white feathers; bill and claws, black. Total length, $12\frac{1}{2}$ inches; wing, $6\frac{7}{8}$; tail, $4\frac{7}{16}$; tarsus, $1\frac{3}{16}$; exposed culmen, $\frac{1}{2}$.

The winter dress of both sexes is white.

40.   Evermann's Ptarmigan.

EVERMANN'S PTARMIGAN.

THIS peculiarly marked and very distinct species has as yet only been obtained on Attu Island, one of the Aleutian chain, situated near the western extremity, and about 1400 miles from Unalaska. It may be restricted entirely to this island. There is no other Ptarmigan known to inhabit any portion of North America which can be mistaken for this bird, and it presents in its coloration but little resemblance to any of the other species. It was first obtained by Professor Evermann, and only nine specimens have as yet been procured. Little or nothing is known of its habits, which, however, doubtless do not differ from those of other Ptarmigan.

LAGOPUS EVERMANNI.

Geographical Distribution.—Attu Island, Aleutian Chain.

Adult Male in Summer.—Forehead, white; top of head and back of neck, black, finely barred with tawny; loral space, breast, and entire upper parts, tertials, innermost secondaries, and upper tail-coverts, black, with faint vermiculations of russet on rump, upper tail-coverts, and edges of tertials; sides of face black and white, mixed; comb over eye, scarlet; white feathers of the winter dress are interspersed among those of the back and upper part of the breast; most of wing-coverts, secondaries, and entire primaries, pure white, with the shafts of the primaries pale brown; tail, clove brown, almost black, with narrow white tips to the feathers; entire under parts, including under tail-coverts, pure white; bill and claws, black. Total length, $13\frac{7}{8}$ inches; wing, $7\frac{1}{2}$; tail, $5\frac{3}{4}$; tarsus, $1\frac{3}{4}$; exposed culmen, $\frac{1}{2}$.

This specimen, as indeed was the case with all those obtained, is not in complete summer dress, as is proved by the few white feathers scattered among the black ones, and also by the white forehead. In the perfect breeding plumage these white feathers would probably be absent.

Adult Female in Summer.—Entire plumage of body, ochraceous, palest on the throat, blotched and barred on the back with black, and the feathers having white tips; on the breast and flanks the black blotches are much fewer, but the black bars are broader, and there are no white tips on the breast feathers, but those on the abdomen and some on the flanks are broadly tipped with white; under tail-coverts, ochraceous, barred with black; the tertials, inner secondaries, and some of the greater wing-coverts, ochraceous, like the back, barred and tipped with white; remainder of wing and primaries, pure white, with the shafts of the latter, pale brown; bill and claws, black. Total length, $12\frac{3}{4}$ inches; wing, $6\frac{9}{16}$; tail, $4\frac{7}{8}$; tarsus, $1\frac{7}{8}$; exposed culmen, $\frac{9}{16}$.

In winter both sexes turn white.

Edwin Sheppard.

41. White-Tailed Ptarmigan.

WHITE-TAILED PTARMIGAN.

AN inhabitant of the high mountain ranges, both of certain parts of the United States and the countries lying to the north of our border, this beautiful bird is not very often met with below the timber line. It is the only species of Ptarmigan having a white tail. It ranges from Alaska through British Columbia, and the Western part of the United States to New Mexico, where it has been obtained at Taos. In certain parts of Idaho, Montana, Wyoming, and Colorado it is not uncommon near the summits of the mountains. It may be regarded as truly an Alpine species. It does not migrate, and wherever found there it breeds, and descends perhaps a few thousand feet when the weather is very severe, but seldom below 6000 or 7000 feet. I have met with this species in the Cascade Range in autumn, where it is usually found in small companies of perhaps half a dozen, occasionally twice this number. They were not what may be called tame, unlike the Willow Grouse in this respect, but were always very uneasy at my presence, and ran about with uplifted tail as if uncertain which way to fly, but when they once got started there seemed to be no farther difficulty in their minds as to the proper direction, which I noticed never led near where I stood. Sometimes I have seen them light on the bare limbs of a stunted tree or large bush at the edge of the timber line, where they stood perfectly motionless for quite a length of time, observing every movement I made, and then suddenly burst away with great speed, uttering a low cackle as they flew. They are very skillful in concealing themselves, either squatting in the snow with only the head exposed to view, or else crouching behind some stone or large bowlder. In summer their peculiar gray plumage assimilates so well to the hue of the ground and the moss-covered stones lying about in all directions that it is next to impossible to perceive them, and at this period, especially during the breeding season, they rarely move when approached, perhaps only going a few feet on one side to avoid being stepped upon.

In winter their white dress makes them so absolutely indistinguishable from the snow that, unless they move, a person could pass close to them and never notice them at all. The nesting season commences in June, and the eggs are deposited in a slight depression in the ground, lined with grass and a few feathers from the bird's breast, or in a patch of short grass pressed down by the hen into a circular shape. These so-called nests are always at a very high elevation, in some localities rarely below 12,000 feet, and eight to ten is the usual number of the eggs. They have a ground color varying from a creamy to a salmon buff, with spots and blotches of reddish and chocolate brown, but not nearly so completely covered with markings as is the case with the eggs of the other species of Ptarmigan. When incubating, the hen leaves the nest with great reluctance, and will often remain when the danger of being trodden upon by both man and beast is imminent, and, when she does move, will go but a little way before she stops and watches the intruder, expressing her disapprobation at having her eggs handled by uttering a low, rolling note. It has been said that instances have occurred when a hen has permitted herself to be lifted from the nest and, when re-

leased, made no effort to fly away, but waited until she
was permitted to return to her charge. But one brood
is raised in a year, and the chicks, when first hatched,
are curiously striped with bands of white and blackish
brown. The hen defends them with great courage, not
hesitating to fly directly into the face of anybody who
may attempt to catch one of her brood, and strikes as violently as she is able with her wings. At other times
she uses all the artifices common to game birds to draw
one away from the vicinity of her young.

By the latter part of August the brood is pretty fully
grown, unless from some cause the birds have been
hatched later than usual. They are delicate at first, and
doubtless many perish from severe weather, or by getting
their downy plumage wet, which generally has a fatal
effect. This Ptarmigan, also called the White, Snow, or
Mountain Quail, by the miners and others who penetrate
its retreats, feeds upon leaves and tender stalks of various plants growing in the Alpine regions amid which
it dwells, also on insects of different kinds, and in
winter on the buds and leaves of firs and pines. Its
flesh is much lighter than that of other Ptarmigan, and is
about as palatable as is theirs, which sometimes is pretty
tasteless. When much hunted the White-tailed Ptarmigan becomes very wild, and it is difficult to approach
it within shot. It makes no extended flights, but
runs on ahead, dodging behind rocks and bushes, stopping at times to watch its pursuer, and occasionally flying a short distance so as just to keep beyond the range
of the gun. If persistently followed for a considerable
period, it is then very apt to remove itself from the locality, at least for a brief period. A solitary bird is not apt
to try and make its escape by flight, and can be flushed
with difficulty, generally trying to steal away quietly,

or else remaining motionless, evidently hoping to escape in that way from being seen. But if several are together they will usually take wing, making a great cackling as they rise and fly off.

The flight of this species is firm and well sustained, consisting of a rapid beating of the wings, succeeded by a sailing movement, and can be continued for a long distance; but, as a rule, the birds alight after proceeding for a few hundred yards. The White-tailed Ptarmigan, like its relatives, appears to be continually in moult. It begins to show a few of the blackish brown vermiculated feathers in March, which appear very conspicuously amid the white plumage. The change from out the winter dress is effected very slowly, and the perfect summer plumage is not assumed until about June. In September it begins to change again, the feathers on the under parts being the first that are replaced with white ones. There is no regularity in this moult, as white feathers appear in different parts of the body after the process has once commenced; but it goes on so deliberately that little difference in the bird's appearance is noticeable for some weeks, save perhaps the general hue is somewhat lighter, and it is quite late in the autumn—perhaps, at times, even the middle of winter—before the pure white dress is completed. During all this period of changing plumage no two individuals are alike. The tail remains white all the year round, and renders the bird very conspicuous during the summer months.

Although, as I have stated, it is rarely seen in the Cascade Mountains in flocks of any size, yet farther south, as in the mountains of Colorado, it associates in companies composed sometimes of a hundred individuals or more. This, however, seems to be an aggregation of birds mostly not fully grown, a number of broods con-

42. White-Tailed Ptarmigan in Winter.

gregated together, but even in these localities I am not aware that these flocks keep unbroken during the winter. It would appear to be more an incident of the breeding season. The males are very pugnacious, and during the period of courtship desperate battles frequently occur when two cocks happen to meet. In winter, when pursued, this Ptarmigan will dive into the snow, and doubtless, like the Ruffed Grouse and other gallinaceous birds, it may be accustomed to enter a snow bank to sleep and obtain protection in that way both from the severity of the weather and from whatever enemies may be prowling amid the lofty heights among which it dwells.

LAGOPUS LEUCURUS.

Geographical Distribution.—High range of mountains from Liard River, British America, and Western United States to New Mexico.

Adult Male.—Upper parts, golden gray or grayish buff, irregularly barred and vermiculated with black; top of head, black, with tips of feathers light brown; lores, black; rest of head and neck, finely barred with black and buff, and feathers tipped with white; cheeks, chin, and throat, white, spotted with black, only sparsely on the throat; breast, barred with black and umber-brown; flanks, similar, but black bars finer and very irregular, and black vermiculations; rest of lower parts, white; legs and toes covered with white feathers; tail, white; bill, black. Total length, about 12½ inches; wing, 6½.

Adult Female.—Resembles the male, but with perhaps more buff. There seems to be, however, very little difference in the coloring of the sexes. Dimensions, about the same as those of the male.

WILD TURKEY.

IN the United States there are at present recognized four different kinds of Wild Turkeys, resembling each other, as would naturally be supposed, in many particulars, but each having its own peculiarities and well-defined limits of dispersion. The present species is the well-known bird of the Eastern portion of the Union, north of Florida, and formerly was much more extensively distributed than it is at the present day. From various causes, but chiefly too much killing, it has entirely disappeared from many localities in which it was formerly abundant, and become greatly lessened in others, and its range is yearly being gradually more restricted, as though the fate that has befallen so many wild creatures would also, in an altogether too brief period, overtake this noble bird, and another name be added to the list of the members of our Fauna that have become extinct. In the Atlantic States, where it formerly was found from southern Maine to Florida, a few are now left in certain parts of Pennsylvania, which is its northern limit, becoming more abundant to the southward. Some are still met with in wooded districts of Ohio, in the southern parts of Michigan and Wisconsin, and the States lying on the west side of the Mississippi to Texas. It is common in the Indian Territory, and not scarce in the Gulf States and parts of Texas. It used to be frequently met with in certain portions of Canada, but if any remain to-day they would probably be found in southwestern Ontario.

•

The Wild Turkey is a bird of the forest, and loves to dwell in the thick portions of the woods, or in the depths of the swamps and similar retreats, where it is far removed from man, and little liable to be disturbed by his attentions. In places where it has not been persecuted by hunters, or frequently shot at, if there are any such remaining at the present day, the Turkey is not apt to be any wilder or more wary than other forest creatures, and it has been known to approach the dwellings and feed among the tame turkeys and other domestic fowl. But when it has learned man's ways, and that his presence means death to any animal within the range of his gun, no more cunning, suspicious, wary animal lives than the Wild Turkey, nor one better able to take care of itself, though too often all its efforts to preserve its life avail nothing against the ingenuity and persistency of its human foe. The nesting season of this splendid bird commences according to the latitude of its habitat, from February, in the southern portion of its range, until June in the northern. The males are polygamous, and everyone is familiar with their pompous strut and attitude during the courting season. The hen hides her nest very carefully as well from the gobbler as from other depredators, for he would not hesitate to make way with both eggs and chicks if he had the chance, and she employs the same route both when approaching and leaving her eggs. The nest is a simple affair situated near some stump or fallen log, in the midst of a clump of bushes or in high grass, in fact in any place where the required concealment can be obtained. The complement of eggs is from seven to twelve; but occasionally two hens will lay in the same nest, and then as many as two dozen have been found. In such a case it would naturally be supposed that both birds would sit together.

The young are very delicate little things and a wetting is almost certainly fatal, and it is a wonder how the mother is able to raise as many as she does. Certainly the task before her is no light one, to guard and protect her brood against the elements as well as all her furred, feathered, and scaly enemies, always on the alert for such a desirable morsel as a chicken turkey. In the early spring at break of day the gobblers are heard calling from some favored roost in the forest. At such times they are exceedingly watchful and suspicious, and the least glimpse of a hunter, or frequently the breaking of a stick under foot, will cause them to fly at once, and it is rare for them to return to the vicinity of that place again during the day. The hens attend these trysting places, and should two gobblers meet they fight desperately, as they are very jealous and ready at all times to defend their fancied prerogatives. Many are shot at this season, as the birds are accustomed to resort to the same roost at night, and when this has been discovered, the hunter either goes near to it during the night and waits for the dawn and light enough to see the sights of his gun, or makes a stealthy stalk until within shot, after the break of day. One brood is raised in a season, but a hen may lay a second complement of eggs, if from any mishap the first clutch has been lost. The eggs are creamy white, finely spotted with reddish brown. At the end of the nesting season the males separate from the females and keep by themselves, reuniting again when they have recovered their pristine vigor. The females lead their young where they can catch insects and such other food as is suitable for them, and each family keeps apart until the young are fairly well-grown, and then several may join together, their number at length being augmented by the returning males.

Although they seem to become attached to a particular locality and rarely stray far from it, yet the birds wander a good deal, especially when gathered together in flocks of any size. A stream of considerable width, lying in their course, proves an obstacle to their farther progress perhaps for several days, during which time the males strut and gobble as if encouraging the young and themselves to undertake the passage. At length they mount to the highest branches overhanging the banks, and launch themselves out over the water, and fly for the opposite shore. Should any fail to make the bank and fall into the water, they spread their tails and swim to land if the distance be not too great. The call note of the Wild Turkey, both the gobble of the male, and the low, soft call of the female, is very like that of the domestic bird, and although there are slight differences, it would take a Turkey itself, or the well-trained ear of an expert, to distinguish them. The food of this bird consists of nuts of various kinds, acorns, such as grow on the different species of oaks; chestnuts, pecan nuts, seeds of many sorts, berries, grapes, insects, and grain. They are very fond of grasshoppers, and it is said that a flock of Turkeys will so systematically traverse and explore a field, that it will be entirely cleared of these insects in a brief period. Turkeys do not migrate in the strict sense of the term, but when food grows scarce from any cause in one section of the country, they naturally will move on, seeking a better land. For this reason Turkeys may at times be scarce in localities usually favorable for them, and to which they have been accustomed to resort in numbers, and again other districts, where they have not been especially abundant, will, from an excess of food supply, suddenly contain large flocks of these birds. They will return, however, to their usual haunts as soon as the conditions become again favorable. The appearance of the Wild Turkey is magnificent as he walks in stately dignity in his native wilds, the sun glancing from his burnished plumage in flashes of emerald and gold, and his erect, graceful, and easy carriage, with head well up, alert to every sound or movement, exhibits him, as he really is, the finest and noblest game bird in the world.

MELEAGRIS SYLVESTRIS.

Geographical Distribution.—From Pennsylvania, where a few possibly survive, to the Gulf States, except Florida, and westward to Wisconsin in the north, and to Texas in the south, in wooded districts.

Adult Male.—General plumage, brilliant metallic, gold, green, bronze, and red reflections, each feather tipped with a band of velvety black; secondaries, bronzy green, barred with whitish; primaries, black, barred with white, the bars reaching the shafts; rump, black, feathers glossed with dark metallic purple; upper tail-coverts, dark chestnut, with metallic red reflections, and barred with black; tail feathers, chestnut barred and vermiculated with black, a subapical broad black band and deep buff tips; head and neck, naked, red; a long bunch of coarse, stiff black bristles is suspended from center of breast; legs, red, spurred; bill, red. Total length, about four feet; wing, 21 inches; tail, 19; weight, from twelve to nearly forty pounds.

Adult Female.—Smaller and with much duller colors, very little of the brilliant metallic hues seen in the male, and without the pendent bunch of bristles.

44. Florida Wild Turkey.

FLORIDA WILD TURKEY.

WHEN I first visited Florida, Wild Turkeys were quite abundant even in the near vicinity of St. Augustine, and ascending the St. John's it was not an unusual thing to see a flock walking sedately along the bank of the river, or on the edge of the woods when these did not come to the water; and not infrequently one would be killed by a bullet from some passenger's rifle, and the boat's nose run against the bank to allow one of the crew to jump ashore and retrieve the game. But in these days, except in the wilder portions of the State, where they are still abundant, they have greatly decreased in numbers, and like their Northern relative, are rapidly disappearing. They were not so excessively shy and wary before they were so persecuted and persistently hunted, and I remember well the first time I ever saw a Florida Turkey. I had been hunting deer on horseback south of St. Augustine, and night coming on we decided to camp for the night, and rode into a clump of trees and palmettoes near which, on the other side, stretched a swamp of considerable extent. As I dismounted from my horse there was a sudden rush and commotion in front, and a flock of Turkeys started away, some to run and a few to take wing. The runners soon disappeared, but the flying birds took refuge in the trees near at hand, and standing motionless, or else slowly walking on the large limbs, looked down upon us as if wondering what kind of intruders we were. They evinced no particular alarm, certainly nothing like that which one of these birds would be apt to show at the present time under similar circumstances.

Rifles and shotguns were quickly made ready, and several of the birds remained with us; the rest of the flock seeking a more secure retreat, where they could indulge their curiosity with less risk to themselves. The appearance of the Florida Turkey is very like the Northern bird, and only an expert would be apt to notice the difference. This chiefly consists in the darker colors generally of the present race, and in having the primaries black with white bars, these last not reaching the shaft, while in those of the Northern bird they go to the shaft of the feather. It is a slight variation, but sufficient to constitute what is considered a geographical race. Turkeys in Florida seem to wander a good deal, perhaps really not more than do those inhabiting other States, but they are abundant at times in one locality, and then will be quite scarce again in the same place. Probably the quantity or absence of food is the main cause of this unsettled phase of their existence, for it is well known that all Turkeys will travel many miles to procure any food they particularly fancy when they know where it is to be obtained. The Florida Turkey goes in small flocks, and keeps to the thick woods and dense swamps. The males can be called like those of the Northern bird, by the imitation of the hen's note in the spring, and they approach the hunter's ambush with all the suspicion and cunning of an old campaigner, urged on by the desire burning in his breast. But with all his eagerness to meet his supposed lady-love, he is watchful of every sight or sound that comes to eye or ear, and is off in a moment if his fears are aroused, disappearing quietly and swiftly as if he had vanished into air. Should two males encounter each other at this season, desperate are the battles that ensue, and should one get a firm hold of the other by the head, he will hang on until his adversary is exhausted, perhaps dead. It is said that a gobbler will caress the dead body of his fallen foe, but I have never witnessed this. The males begin to gobble in February and nesting commences in March. The usual depression is made beneath a palmetto and lined with grass, leaves, and similar rubbish, and usually about ten eggs are laid, exactly similar in appearance to those of the Northern Wild Turkey. The chicks remain with the mother until full grown, when they may unite with other families if they happen to meet, and in the autumn the males join them. Their habits do not differ from those of the other races, and the Florida bird, though not so brilliant perhaps, is also a magnificent creature.

MELEAGRIS SYLVESTRIS OSCEOLA.

Geographical Distribution.—Florida.

Adult Male.—Resembles *M. sylvestris*, but much darker in the general hue of the plumage; there is a great deal of brilliant metallic coloring observable in different shades of bronze, greens, and fiery reds, but the chief difference between this race and other Wild Turkeys consists in the markings of the primaries and secondaries, though to a less extent in the latter. The primaries and outer secondaries are brownish black, with narrow broken bars of white that do not reach the shaft of the feather, while the inner secondaries are grayish brown, apparently without bars, but vermiculated with dark brown on the inner web. The dimensions are about the same as the Northern Wild Turkey.

Adult Female.—Like the male, but smaller and less brilliant in coloration.

ELLIOT'S RIO GRANDE TURKEY.

THIS handsome race of the Wild Turkey is restricted, so far as is known at present, to the lowlands of eastern Mexico and southern Texas, ranging not farther south than Vera Cruz nor north of the Brazos River, or about ten degrees of latitude. This is the dispersion given to the bird by its describer, my friend Mr. George B. Sennett. It is a dweller of the woodlands and is not met with much, if any, above an altitude of 2000 feet. While having the general appearance of the eastern Wild Turkey it differs from that and all the other races in many particulars; and the hen is unlike that of any other species or race of Turkeys known at the present day. No evidence of its intergrading with the common species has yet been obtained, but it is expected that it would interbreed with that bird wherever the limits of their dispersion came in contact. It has always been confounded with the Common Wild Turkey, and although its peculiar coloring and marking had been observed and commented on by many ornithologists it was not until lately that sufficient specimens were obtained, and its restricted habitat known, to prove its claim to be considered as a distinct race. Its habits are the same as those already described in the articles on the other races, and in beauty and brilliancy of its metallic coloring, as well as in size, it is not inferior to any of the Wild Turkeys inhabiting Mexico and the rest of the continent lying to the northward. The female varies greatly from the male, and in fact she is differ-

45. Elliot's Rio Grande Turkey.

ently marked from the hens of all other species of Turkeys; sufficiently characteristic in my opinion to give the bird specific rank, although I retain its subspecific nomenclature.

MELEAGRIS SYLVESTRIS ELLIOTI.

Habitat.—Lowlands of southern Texas and eastern Mexico, from the Brazos River to Vera Cruz not above 2000 feet of elevation. Northeastern Mexico.

Adult Male.—Head, neck, mantle, upper wing-coverts, and breast resemble those of the eastern Wild Turkey, *M. sylvestris;* back and rump, jet black, with, in certain lights, a silvery gray bar near the ends of all the feathers, and a narrower one on the tip, both with roseate reflections; upper tail-coverts, broadly tipped with ochraceous buff (and this is the general color of the lower rump and upper tail-coverts), remaining parts, chestnut, irregularly crossed with black lines, succeeded by a black bar with metallic copper bronze reflections; back and rump, jet black; lower back, with a coppery metallic bar near the tip of the feathers; tail, mottled with pale chestnut and black, a black band near the end and the tip ochraceous buff; under tail-coverts, black, with metallic green, bronze, and red reflections, and broadly tipped with ochraceous buff. Wing, 21 inches; tail, 19; tarsus, 6¼.

Young Male has the feathers of the breast, under parts, flanks, back, and rump conspicuously tipped with ochraceous buff.

Adult Female.—Smaller than male, general hue, black, with the metallic iridescent hues of the male present on the back, wings, and under surface; feathers of the entire upper parts have black bars near the ends and grayish tips, becoming broader on the lower back and rump; feathers of under surface tipped with pale buff; upper and under tail-coverts and tail resemble those of the male, and all except the under coverts have very pale ochraceous buff tips.

MEXICAN TURKEY.

FROM this bird came the domesticated race of Turkeys. It is a common species on the table-lands of Mexico, and within our borders is found in southern and western Texas, New Mexico, and Arizona at an altitude of from 3000 to 10,000 feet above the sea. It is a bird of the highlands and mountainous regions, and is rather larger and heavier than the Wild Turkey of the Atlantic States. The light rump with the broad white borders to the feathers, makes it conspicuously different from all its allies, and is one of the characteristic marks of the domestic bird. I found this species very abundant upon the highlands in southern New Mexico near the borders of Arizona, and met with them in flocks of considerable size. They had all the habits of the Eastern bird, and were wary and difficult to approach. It was late in the autumn and the piñon nuts were abundant, and the birds kept closely to the groves of the trees which were covered with these nuts, and apparently fed exclusively upon them. Their flesh was so highly scented by this food that, when the Turkeys were over the fire, they perfumed the camp with a most appetizing odor, and I know no better dish than a roasted Mexican Turkey that has been fed on piñon nuts. About three miles from one of our camps was a place where the Turkeys were in the habit of roosting, and we visited the spot several times. On the first occasion I left camp about half an hour before sundown, and came near the roosting place just at dark. The Turkeys had selected a

46. Mexican Turkey.

·

grove of lofty pines, the first branches of which were too high for any missile to reach and do execution upon so large a bird, save a bullet from a rifle. As my companion and myself quietly sat upon the ground a quarter of a mile away, waiting for the daylight to leave the sky, we heard the Turkeys flying into the trees, and gobbling at intervals as they settled themselves for the night. Soon darkness spread her veil around us, and all sounds from the roost ceased, and we commenced cautiously to draw near our objective point.

Soon we could distinguish the trees in which we knew the birds were, but the branches were so far from the ground that at first nothing could be seen that resembled a Turkey. Gradually we drew near until we stood beneath the overspreading limbs and close to the trunk of the tree each had selected. No movement or sound from above indicated that we had been observed by the watchful birds, and now to our eyes, grown more accustomed to the obscurity, some clumps and bunches appeared upon the branches toward the sky. It was almost impossible to tell what these were, whether Turkeys squatting on the limbs, or masses of moss or foliage. But the only way to find out was to shoot at them, which we did. At the crack of the rifles came numerous *pit-pits* and a stray gobble as the aroused birds moved upon their perches and questioned this unusual uproar. Their movements disclosed their forms without mistake, and soon there was added to the noise of the firearms, and the calls of the now thoroughly startled birds, the crash of the falling Turkeys striking the limbs as they descended, and then the heavy " thump " as the body reached the ground. For a short time confusion reigned. Unharmed birds began to leave the trees, and the whir and beat of their wings

sounded above the various cries they uttered, and occasionally one wounded, but not entirely incapacitated
from escaping, would drop to the ground and the
rapid " pats " of its swiftly moving feet could be heard
upon the dead leaves as it ran quickly from the scene.
The roost, however, was very extensive and continued a
long way up the cañon, and the birds not in the imme-
diate vicinity did not desert their posts.   Picking up the
dead birds, a few of which were quite a heavy enough
load for two men, we were glad when we could transfer
them from our own backs to those of our horses, which
were waiting for us about half a mile away.   This Turkey is very strong upon the wing, rises without difficulty,
and continues its flight frequently for long distances.
It alights either upon the ground or in the trees, but if
the former, runs with great speed until a place of concealment is gained.   While not uncommon in the districts named within our limits, this species is much more
numerous in Mexico, where it goes as far south as Vera
Cruz.   The hen attends solely to the hatching of the
eggs and rearing of the young, hiding them away from
the male, who cannot be trusted either with them or a
knowledge of their location.   The nest is a depression in
the ground, lined with grass, weeds, and leaves, and carefully concealed amid bushes or grass.   The eggs are
creamy white, finely and thickly dotted with reddish
brown.   The food of this bird consists of acorns and
various nuts that are found in those southern latitudes,
especially those of the piñon tree, also insects of all kinds,
and grain when it happens to be grown in the vicinity
of their habitats.

This Turkey was carried to some of the West Indies
Islands early in the sixteenth century, and then to
Europe, especially England and France, and in 1573 had

become quite numerous and was freely used as an article of food. In the days of the Emperors of Mexico Montezuma possessed extensive Zoölogical Gardens, and many of these birds were given to the wild beasts for food. Certainly they had no fault to find with the fare served to them. The Mexican Turkey, as I have said, is possibly a somewhat larger bird, and exhibits a good many of the metallic tints of its Eastern relative, yet it can hardly be regarded as equally beautiful, as the white on the rump detracts greatly from the general brilliancy of its appearance. Still it is a magnificent game bird, and is worthy to be compared with its rivals of the Eastern and Northern portions of the United States.

MELAGRIS GALLOPAVO.

Geographical Distribution.—Western Texas to Arizona. Table-lands of Mexico.

Adult Male.—Rather larger than the average common Wild Turkey, and with fully as much of the brilliant metallic coloring so conspicuous in its better known relative. The principal differences exhibited by the present bird are the upper tail-coverts, which are broadly tipped with white, barred posteriorly by a band of black, the rest of the feathers being metallic bronze ; tail, very dark brown, especially toward the tip, spotted and vermiculated with black and tipped with white ; feathers on lower part of flanks and under tail-coverts are also tipped with white; the primaries are white, barred with blackish brown, apparently more white visible on the webs than of the other color; head and neck, bare, red. Measurements and weights vary considerably among individuals, and those given for the common Wild Turkey will answer for this one also. There is a long bunch of stiff black bristles pendent from the chest.

Adult Female.—Smaller and with much less of the metallic coloring, and without the pendent bristles or " beard."

APPENDIX.

KEYS TO THE FAMILIES, SUBFAMILIES, GENERA, AND SPECIES.

KEY TO THE FAMILIES.

(Referring only to North American Species.)

A. Head feathered, tarsi bare, or partly or completely feathered. No spurs on tarsi. Plumage not iridescent. } PARTRIDGES AND GROUSE. *Tetraonidæ.*

B. Head and upper part of neck, bare. Tarsi always bare. Spurs on tarsi of male. Plumage iridescent. } WILD TURKEYS. *Phasianidæ.*

KEY TO SUBFAMILIES.

A. No spurs on legs.

   a. Nasal fossæ and tarsi bare. Sides of toes not pectinated. Cutting edge of mandible more or less distinctly serrated near the tip. } AMERICAN PARTRIDGES. *Odontophorinæ* Page 19.

   b. Nasal fossæ densely feathered, Tarsi and toes partly, or completely covered with feathers. Sides of toes pectinated. Cutting edge of mandible not serrated. } GROUSE AND PTARMIGAN. *Tetraoninæ.* Page 74.

B. With spurs on tarsi of male. } WILD TURKEYS. *Meleagrinæ.* Page 172.

FAMILY TETRAONIDÆ.

THIS family contains the Quails, Partridges, and Grouse, and has its representatives in nearly every portion of the world. It has been subjected by different ornithologists to varying treatment and has at times been divided into many subfamilies, but three have always seemed to me quite sufficient, two of which are represented in North America. The three are: *Perdicinæ*, containing the Quails and Partridges of the Old World, having no representative in the Western Hemisphere; *Odontophorinæ*, the American Partridges, natives of the New World unrepresented in the Old World; and *Tetraoninæ*, the Grouse and Ptarmigan found in both Hemispheres.

They are all game birds, in the sense the sportsman understands the term, and wherever their habitat may be, whether the elevated plateaus or gloomy defiles of high mountain ranges, or the plains and prairies of level lands, or the forests and thickets of the more attractive portions of the earth, the members of this family always exhibit the peculiar qualities found so eminently among gallinaceous birds, and afford the sport that so endears them to the hunter's heart.

The New World possesses some of the largest and finest species of the family, many of which at one time were found within its limits in extraordinary abundance, and although they now exist in lessened numbers, and many districts in which they formerly abounded will know them no more forever, yet with proper laws, rightly enforced, a remnant may be saved for succeeding generations.

SUBFAMILY ODONTOPHORINÆ.

THIS division of the family TETRAONIDÆ comprises the American Partridges, which differ from those of the Eastern Hemisphere in having the mandible notched on either side, although in some species this is hardly apparent. The group throughout the Western Hemisphere consists of about nine genera and between forty and fifty species, of which in North America, according to my views, five genera and thirteen species and subspecies are found. They are birds of shapely, sometimes gracefully formed bodies, and with an attractive plumage, which indeed, in some species, may be called beautiful. The American Partridges go in coveys generally consisting of one family, but some species, notably of the genus LOPHORTYX, gather at certain seasons in packs, often of five or six hundred individuals, resembling in this respect the Prairie Grouse of different species. The North American Partridges, excepting perhaps those that "pack," are game in the highest sense of the term, lie well to the dog, and afford the greatest sport in the field. Brave little birds, with well-sharpened wits, fertile in resources that promise to insure their own safety, and wide-awake to seize every advantage that offers for their own benefit. Gallant "Bob White" and his near relatives certainly have a warm place in the heart of every true sportsman in the land.

KEY TO THE GENERA.

A. Claws moderate, normal.

   a. Crest, moderate, inconspicuous. } BOB WHITES. *Colinus.* Page 19.

   b. Crest very long, slender, of two feathers. } PLUMED PARTRIDGES. *Orcortyx.* Page 41.

   c. Crest full, conspicuous. } SCALED PARTRIDGES. *Callipepla.* Page 49.

   d. Crest recurved, of several feathers, enlarged at extremity. } HELMETED PARTRIDGES. *Lophortyx.* Page 55.

B. Claws very long. } MASSENA PARTRIDGES. *Cyrtonyx.* Page 69.

GENUS COLINUS

(Latin *Colinus*, synonymous with the Greek ὄρτυξ, *ortyx*, a quail).

Colinus Less. Man. d'Ornith., vol. ii., 1828, p. 190. Type *Tetrao virginianus*, Linn.

Body short, rounded; feathers of crown slightly rounded and erectile, but not forming a true crest. Tail about three-fifths length of wing. Sexes alike, save in the color of throats and superciliary stripes.

Two species and two subspecies of this genus inhabit North America north of Mexico. Closely allied in habits and appearance three of them might easily be confounded by one not an expert, but the fourth, *C. ridgwayi*, hardly called with propriety a North American species, differs completely in the color of its plumage from the others.

KEY TO THE SPECIES.

A. Adult Males.—Lower parts, white, irregularly barred with black.
  a. Throat, white.
    a'. Band on breast.
      a''. Breast band, light chestnut, inner } BOB WHITE.
        edges of tertials, deep buff.   } *C. virginianus.*

      b''. Breast band, pale cinnamon ; inner } TEXAN BOB
        edges of tertials, buffy white.   } WHITE.
                                               } *C. v. texanus.*

    b'. No band on breast.   } FLORIDA BOB
                                               } WHITE.
                                               } *C. v. floridanus.*

B. Adult Male.—Lower parts, cinnamon-   } MASKED BOB
  rufous.   Throat, black.   } WHITE.
                                               } *C. ridgwayi.*

GENUS OREORTYX

(Greek, ὄρος, *oros*, a mountain; + ὄρτυξ, *ortyx*, a quail).

Oreortyx, Baird. B. North Am., 1858, p. 642. Type *Ortyx
picta.*, Dougl.

Head with a long, slender crest, consisting of two feathers, either
standing upright or inclining slightly backward. Tail broad,
rounded, almost hidden by upper coverts. Tarsus equal to
middle toe and claw.

One species and two subspecies of this genus are recognized,
but there is so very slight a difference between the subspecies
that a close examination is required to separate them, especially
if the locality of the specimens is unknown. They are among
the most brilliantly plumaged members of the family and of a
larger size and greater weight than the other North American
Partridges. Strictly mountain dwellers, they are found in the
summer at very high elevations. Their coloring is peculiar, being massed in large areas and of strongly contrasting hues.
There is considerable difference in the appearance of the sexes,
the female being less gaudily attired and with a much shorter
crest.

KEY TO THE SPECIES.

A. Crest very long and mostly straight.

   a. Above: deep olive-brown from crest to end of tail-coverts.   MOUNTAIN PARTRIDGE. *O. pictus.*

   b. Above: hind-neck and upper back grayish blue.   PLUMED PARTRIDGE. *O. p. plumiferus.*

   c. Above: ashy brown with slight olive-wash.   SAN PEDRO PARTRIDGE. *O. p. confinis.*

The differences between the last bird and the *O. p. plumiferus*, as given by its describer, are so very slight, viz. : " grayer upper parts and thicker bill," that an ornithologist would naturally hesitate before giving it any separate rank, even a subspecific one, until he found characters more decisive and important, that would enable the bird to be recognized from its fellows. Relative proportions of bills, unless very unusual, are notoriously unreliable, and prove generally to be a most unsatisfactory foundation on which to base specific or subspecific forms, and slight shades of color are not much more to be depended on.

GENUS CALLIPEPLA

(Greek, καλλιπεπλος, *Kallipeplos*, beautifully arrayed).

Callipepla, Wagler. Isis., 1832, p. 277. Type, *C. strenua*, Wagl. = *Ortyx squamatus*, Vig.

Crest full, and short, of two colors blending with feathers of the crown. No distinction in plumage of sexes.

I have included but one species and one subspecies in this genus, contrary to the arrangement of the A. O. U. check list, for I cannot satisfy myself that birds so essentially different as the Scaled Partridges, and those represented by Gambel's, the California Partridge, etc., can properly be placed in the same genus. The crests are entirely different in structure, that of the Scaled Partridge being more like that of Bob White and its allies, while those of Gambel's Partridge, and its relatives, are unlike any seen in the family. The sexes of the Blue Partridge also are indistinguishable from each other in plumage, while those of Gambel's, etc., are very different in appearance. Generic terms are, as I well know, often arbitrary, and sometimes most artificial, but in this instance I cannot but think that these birds are more properly placed in separate genera. It would be impossible to define a single genus to contain them both, without using terms, so far as the crests and plumage of the sexes are concerned, that would contradict each other.

KEY TO THE SPECIES.

A. Crest short, blending with crown feathers.

a. No chestnut patch on belly. } SCALED PARTRIDGE. *C. squamata.*

b. Chestnut patch on belly. } CHESTNUT-BELLY SCALED PARTRIDGE. *C. s. castaneigastra.*

GENUS LOPHORTYX

(Greek λόφος, *lophos*, a crest ; + ὄρτυξ, *ortux*, a quail).

Lophortyx, Bonp. Geog., and Comp. List, 1838, p. 42. Type *Tetrao californicus*, Shaw.

Crest recurved, composed of several overlapping feathers, lengthened, upright, widening from base to tip ; fewer and smaller in the female. Tarsus shorter than middle toe and claw. Sexes dissimilar in plumage.

The two species and one subspecies belonging to this genus are the most graceful in carriage and beautiful in plumage of the North American Partridges. The body is well proportioned to the size of the bird, and the variegated dress and peculiar swaying crest combine to present creatures of singular attractiveness. Loath to take wing, preferring to run so long as escape is possible by that method, they lack, to a certain degree, what sportsmen are accustomed to regard as game qualities, and by always indulging in these habits are particularly exasperating to both man and dog. They are accustomed at certain periods to assemble in large flocks, sometimes of several hundreds, and are very abundant in the countries they inhabit. I have, under the genus CALLIPEPLA, given my reasons why I have departed from the arrangement in the Check List and separated these birds from the Scaled Partridges generically. In my opinion the characters are too important to be classed subgenerically, and are entitled to a full generic standing. In fact, there is very little in common either in structure or habits, between the two groups of birds. The only trait possessed by both, to a superlative degree, is that of putting their faith in their legs, instead of, as would be more natural, in their wings. In all other respects they are very unlike.

KEY TO THE SPECIES.

A. Crest lengthened, recurved, elevated, distinct from crown feathers.

    a. Flanks olive-brown, streaked with white.

        a'. Upper parts smoky brown; inner edges of tertials deep buff. — CALIFORNIA PARTRIDGE. *L. californicus.*

        b'. Upper parts grayish brown, inner edges of tertials whitish. — VALLEY PARTRIDGE. *L. c. vallicola.*

    b. Flanks rich chestnut streaked with white. — GAMBEL'S PARTRIDGE. *L. gambeli.*

GENUS CYRTONYX

(Greek κυρτός, *kurtos*, crooked; + ὄνυξ, *onux*, claw).

Cyrtonyx, Gould. Mon., Odont., pt. 1. 1844, pl. vii. Type *Ortyx massena*, Less. = *O. montezuma*, Vig.

Crest full, soft depressed, covering the occiput. Tail almost hidden by the coverts. Bill stout; tarsus shorter than middle toe and claw, the latter greatly developed.

Two species are included in this genus, both of which are essentially Mexican, the present one only coming within our borders. They are remarkable for the fantastic coloring of the head, short tail, and long claws, as well as for their unsuspicious dispositions, which have earned for them the soubriquet of " Fool quail." The species found in the Southern United States is not very abundant anywhere, and will probably soon be very much less so, as making but little effort to escape their pursuers, the members of a flock, when met with, usually all fall victims to their misplaced confidence in man's forbearance.

SUBFAMILY TETRAONINÆ.

THIS subfamily contains the Grouse of the world, consisting of those birds which have the legs and feet more or less feathered, such as the Ruffed Grouse feathered to the heel, the Prairie Grouse and their allies feathered to the toes, and Ptarmigan with both legs and toes completely hidden by feathers. With the exception of the Turkeys this subfamily comprises the largest known species of gallinaceous birds, and is fairly well distributed over North America and the western half of the Eastern Hemisphere. The larger number of species with their subspecies are found in North America between the Arctic Sea and the northern boundary of Mexico, and the two great oceans that line the eastern and western shores. The American species which inhabit the prairies are met with in coveys usually composed of from a dozen to twenty individuals, but at certain seasons of the year, generally late in the autumn, are accustomed to congregate in flocks often of hundreds, and are then exceedingly wild and wary. The forest-loving species are generally found in small companies, the covey usually consisting of a single family, and the birds never gather together in such enormous numbers as do those inhabiting the plains. The flesh of the species dwelling upon the prairies is mostly dark, while that of the forest-loving birds, with one or two exceptions, is white. The flesh of all furnishes most excellent food, save perhaps that of the Sage Cock, and at certain seasons, the Spruce Grouse, which is bitter and unsavory, caused by the particular leaves on which the birds feed. The American species, according to my views, are divided into seven genera and twenty-five species and subspecies.

KEY TO THE GENERA.

A. Legs feathered wholly, or in part.

    a. Legs bare from the heel downward.
        RUFFED GROUSE.
        Bonasa.
        Page 74.

    b. Legs feathered to the toes.
      a'. Tail square at tip.

        a''. Tail feathers 20. Air sacs present.
        DUSKY GROUSE.
        Dendragapus.
        Page 90.

        b''. Tail feathers 16. Air sacs absent.
        SPRUCE GROUSE.
        Canachites.
        Page 100.

      b'. Tail rounded of 18 rather stiff feathers. Tufts of lengthened feathers over air sacs.
        PRAIRIE HENS.
        Tympanuchus.
        Page 110.

      c'. Tail pointed, of 18 soft feathers, central pair longest. No tufts over air sacs.
        SHARP-TAILED GROUSE.
        Pediœcetes.
        Page 123.

      d'. Tail pointed, stiff, of 20 filamentous feathers. Breast feathers hair-like.
        COCK-OF-THE PLAINS.
        Centrocercus.
        Page 136.

B. Legs and toes covered with feathers.
        PTARMIGAN.
        Lagopus.
        Page 142.

GENUS BONASA

(Greek βοναϭα, Latin *bonasus*, a bison. The bird's drumming resembles a bison's bellow).

Bonasa, Steph. Gen. Zoöl., vol. xi., 1819, p. 298. Type *Tetrao umbellus*, Linn.

Head crested, rudimentary air sac covered by a tuft of broad, soft, glossy feathers. Tail broad, long, rounded, fan-shaped.

Legs bare from heel, scutellated in front. Carriage upright, dignified.

One species and three subspecies are recognized of this genus in North America and threè allied species (*Genus Tetrastes*), in the Eastern Hemisphere. They are strictly birds of the woods and thickets, exceedingly cunning and wary, strong of wing and fruitful in expedients to foil the hunter and his four-footed ally, and secure their own escape. The flight is powerful and well sustained, and when startled the birds rise with such a whirring noise that, on a calm day, it resounds through the woods like distant thunder. The flesh is white and palatable, and the species, from their thoroughly gamelike ways and habits, are justly esteemed as perhaps the most gallant and desirable of our native gallinaceous birds.

KEY TO THE SPECIES.

A. Upper parts rusty ; tail usually without gray markings.

　a. Pale above, markings on lower parts in- ⎫ RUFFED GROUSE.
　　distinct. Tail yellowish brown or och- ⎬   *B. umbellus.*
　　raceous. ⎭

　b. Dark above, markings on lower part very ⎫ SABINE'S GROUSE.
　　distinct. Tail rust color or reddish. ⎭   *B. u. sabini.*

B. Upper parts mostly or entirely gray. Tail gray.

　a. Size large.   ⎫ CANADIAN
　　　　　　　　　　　　　　　　　 ⎬ RUFFED GROUSE.
　　　　　　　　　　　　　　　　　 ⎭   *B. u. togata.*

　b. Size small.   ⎫ GRAY RUFFED
　　　　　　　　　　　　　　　　　 ⎬   GROUSE.
　　　　　　　　　　　　　　　　　 ⎬   *B. u. umbel-*
　　　　　　　　　　　　　　　　　 ⎭   *loides.*

GENUS DENDRAGAPUS

(Greek δενδρον, *drendron*, a tree; +ἀγαπαω, *agapao*, to love).

Dendragapus, Elliot. Proc. Acad. Nat. Sci. Phil., 1864, p. 23. Type *Tetrao obscurus*, Say.

Head slightly crested. Tail long, composed of twenty broad feathers, square at tip. Air sacs on neck. Size large.

The single species and its two subspecies, comprising this genus, are fine large birds with white flesh, strictly inhabitants

of the forests, and are found only in the western portions of
North America amid the high mountain ranges. By having dis-
tensible sacs of bare skin upon the sides of the neck, and a tail
consisting of twenty broad feathers, these birds cannot properly
be included in the same genus with the Spruce Grouse, *C. canadensis* and *C. franklini*, which have no air sacs, and only sixteen
rectrices in the tail. These characters are in my opinion strictly
generic and too important and conspicuous to permit the two
groups to be separated only subgenerically, but are as striking
and trenchant as any that separate these birds themselves from
those in other genera of the subfamily.

KEY TO THE SPECIES.

A. Under parts of adult males, mostly slate
color.

   a. Tail with distinct gray band at tip.

      a'. General colors, light. Tail band very } DUSKY GROUSE.
broad. }   *D. obscurus.*

      b'. General colors, dark, almost black. } SOOTY GROUSE.
Tail band narrow. }   *D. o. fuligi-*
}   *nosus.*

   b. Tail without band at tip. } RICHARDSON'S
}   GROUSE.
}   *D. o. richard-*
}   *soni.*

GENUS CANACHITES

(Greek, κavaχεω, *kanacheo*, to be noisy).

Canachites, Stejn. Proc. U. S. Nat. Mus., vol. viii., 1885, p. 410.
Type, *Tetrao canadensis*, Linn.

    Head without crest. Tail moderately long, nearly square at
tip, composed of sixteen feathers. No air sacs on sides of neck.
Toes naked, scaly, and fringed along the sides. Size small.

    Two species only are included in this genus, the common
Spruce or Canada Grouse, and Franklin's Grouse, the latter
dwelling on the high mountain ranges of the western side of
North America. They are quite different in their pattern of
coloration, and the males are characteristically marked and
easily distinguishable.

KEY TO THE SPECIES.

A. Under parts of adult male, mostly black.

 a. Upper tail-coverts narrowly tipped with grayish white. } CANADA GROUSE. *C. canadensis.*

 b. Upper tail-coverts broadly tipped with pure white. } FRANKLIN'S GROUSE. *C. franklini.*

GENUS TYMPANUCHUS

(Latin *Tympanum*, a drum; +*nucha*, neck).

Tympanuchus, Gloger. Gemeinutzig, Hand- und Hilfsbuch, Naturg., 1842, p. 396. Type, *Tetrao cupido*, Linn.

Air sacs on sides of neck, above which arise tufts of winglike, lengthened, more or less acuminated, feathers. Head crested. Tarsi rather scantily feathered to the toes, the latter webbed at base. Tail short, rounded, consisting of eighteen feathers. Size large, sexes similar.

The Prairie Hens are divided into three species and one sub-species, constituting a well-marked and distinct group of the sub-family, with characteristics that easily give them recognition among their allies. They are essentially birds of the plains, although they do not hesitate to perch upon the limbs of trees, fences, or any support that may be most convenient at the time. They go usually in coveys, generally consisting of a single family, but in the autumn are accustomed to gather in enormous packs and then are very difficult of approach. Formerly abundant over much of eastern North America, they are now confined to the prairie countries of the west and south, and the island of Martha's Vineyard on the eastern coast. Throughout their dispersion there is little or no difference in the habits of the various races.

KEY TO THE SPECIES.

A. Winglike tufts of feathers on the sides of neck.

 a. Neck tufts pointed. Size large.

  a'. Scapulars without conspicuous white terminal spot. Neck tufts very long. } PRAIRIE HEN. *T. americanus.*

b' Scapulars with conspicuous white ter- } HEATH HEN.
minal spot, neck tufts short. } *T. cupido.*

b. Neck tufts rounded or almost square.
Size small.

a'. Without band of cinnamon rufous at
base of neck.
} LESSER PRAIRIE HEN. *T. pallidi-cinctus.*

b'. With band of cinnamon rufous at base
of neck.
} ATTWATER'S PRAIRIE HEN. *T. a. attwateri.*

GENUS PEDIŒCETES

(Greek, πεδίον, *pedion*, a plain; + οἰκέτης, *oiketes*, an inhabitant).

Pediœcetes, Baird. B. North Am., 1868, p. 625. Type, *Tetrao phasianellus.* Linn.

No tufts of feathers above air sacs. Head slightly crested. Tarsi and base of toes feathered, the feathers in one species covering the latter, reaching in hairlike webs to the claws. Toes scutellated transversely above, fringed on sides with horny comb-like processes. Tail of eighteen feathers, soft, pointed, with the median pair longest and rather square at tip. Size large, sexes similar.

One species and two subspecies comprise this genus of the Sharp-tailed Grouse. Terrestrial in their habits, yet not averse to perching on branches of trees and other convenient supports like their allies, the Prairie Hens. They are more shy in their dispositions than the members of the genus *Tympanuchus*, and are not so fond of loitering about the farm buildings, but prefer wild districts and man's absence. They go in small coveys for the greater part of the year, but like other prairie dwellers, congregate in immense packs, in the autumn. They are fine birds, with many game qualities, and are found in the more central portions of North America from the Arctic Sea to New Mexico.

KEY TO THE SPECIES.

A. Median tail feathers extending beyond the rest.

a. General plumage mostly black and white.
} SHARP-TAILED GROUSE. *P. phasianel-lus.*

b. General plumage lighter, pale brown predominating.

a'. Ground color of upper parts grayish clay color, with but little of a rusty tinge. } COLUMBIAN SHARP-TAILED GROUSE. *P. p. columbianus.*

b'. Ground color of upper parts rusty or ochraceous. } PRAIRIE SHARP-TAILED GROUSE. *P. p. campestris.*

GENUS CENTROCERCUS

(Greek κεντρον, *kentron*, a spine; + κερκος, *kerkos*, tail).

Centrocercus, Swain. Faun. Bor. Amer., 1831, pp. 358, 496. Type, *Tetrao urophasianus*, Bonp.

No crest. Enormous air sacs present of irregular contour, fringed above by hairlike filaments, below covered with horny white feathers like scales, varying with the seasons according to the wear of the feathers. Tail very long, composed of twenty stiff, narrow, graduated acuminate feathers. Bill large and strong. Tarsi feathered to the toes. Sexes similar in plumage, but of greatly disproportionate size; the female being very much the smaller.

But one species is contained in this genus, the remarkable Sage Cock, or Cock-of-the-Plains, with the exception of the Capercailzie of the Old World, the largest species of the subfamily, indeed almost equaling in bulk that giant of the Grouse Tribe. It inhabits the sage plains of the West, subsisting mainly upon the leaves of that plant, which give to the flesh an exceedingly bitter taste. It is exclusively a terrestrial species, and it has a vigorous, well-sustained flight, consisting of several rapid beats of the pinions, succeeded by sailings with the wings held stiff and motionless. It is an unique species, and has no particularly near relative. It goes in flocks, and at times exhibits no fear of man.

GENUS LAGOPUS

(Greek λαγοπους, *lagopus*, hare foot).

Lagopus, Briss. Ornith., vol. i., 1760, p. 181. Type, *Tetrao lagopus*, Linn.

Tarsi and toes densely feathered. Tail rather short, slightly rounded, consisting of fourteen feathers, but counting the two long upper median coverts, sixteen. Sexes dissimilar, both turning white in winter.

Ptarmigan dwell in high latitudes, and are found in the Arctic regions of both hemispheres, one species, *L. lagopus*, being an inhabitant of both the Old and New Worlds. They are recognizable from other grouse by having the toes as well as the legs covered with feathers, sometimes the claws even being hidden. Also, all the species save one (*Lagopus scoticus*), turn white in winter, and the difference between that and the summer dress is so great, and the latter is retained for so brief a period, that the plumage appears to be always in a transient state, and the birds are robed for the greater portion of the year in a piebald dress. There are recognized at present four species and six subspecies inhabiting North America, and several other distinct species which are natives of the Old World. While possessing characteristic traits, which render them easily recognizable from each other, when the specimens are before the observer, there is, nevertheless, such a uniformity of color and markings among a number of the species and their races, that it is no easy matter to indicate the difference so as to clearly define them to the comprehension of any-one who has not seen the specimens. Therefore the accompanying *key*, while it gives the most marked differences observable, may fail to be of equal assistance to those entirely unfamiliar with Ptarmigan as are the keys for the other species of gallinaceous game birds.

KEY TO THE SPECIES.

A. Tail always black.
- *a*. No black loral space in male.

     a'. Shafts of secondaries, white. } WILLOW PTAR-MIGAN. *L. lagopus.*

     b'. Shafts of secondaries, black.* } ALLEN'S PTAR-MIGAN. *L. l. alleni.*

- *b*. Black loral space in male.

     a'. Male in summer with black blotches on back and scapulars, vermiculations coarse. Ground color grayish brown. Female, bright ochraceous, spotted and barred with black. } ROCK PTAR-MIGAN. *L. rupestris.*

     *See remarks in article on this bird, page 149.

b'. Male in summer, above less coarsely barred. Female chiefly black, varied with grayish buff. } REINHARDT'S PTARMIGAN. *L. r. reinhardti.*

c'. Male in summer, brownish gray above, vermiculated and spotted with black. Female black, deep buff, and grayish white. } WELCH'S PTARMIGAN. *L. r. welchi.*

d'. Male in summer, dark russet above, finely vermiculated with black with occasional black blotches. } NELSON'S PTARMIGAN. *L. r. nelsoni.*

e'. Male in summer, above tawny ochraceous, russet, and gray, finely vermiculated and dotted with black. } TURNER'S PTARMIGAN. *L. r. atkensis.*

f'. Male in summer, raw-umber, above tinged with russet, and finely vermiculated and blotched with black. } TOWNSEND'S . PTARMIGAN. *L.r. townsendi.*

g'. Male in summer, chiefly black and white, vermiculated with tawny. } EVERMANN'S PTARMIGAN. *L. evermanni.*

B. Tail always white. } WHITE-TAILED PTARMIGAN. *L. leucurus.*

FAMILY PHASIANIDÆ.

THIS is one of the largest, and, regarded as a source of food supply to man, the most important family of birds. It contains between eighty and ninety species, with the exception of our Wild Turkeys all natives of the Old World, and among its members are found some of the most gorgeously plumaged creatures known in the class of birds. Some of these which might be mentioned are the species of LOPHOPHORUS from India and Asia, resplendent with metallic hues of gold and fiery red, changing to blues and greens of varying intensity; the ocellated spurred fowl of the genus POLYPLECTRUM, with wings and tail covered with oblong disks like great eyes, of metallic blues, purples, and greens; of the various graceful and highly-colored members of the genus PHA-SIANUS, and many others, constituting an assemblage of remarkable species difficult to rival. In North America the family is only represented by the common Wild Turkey and its three races, and its beautiful relative the Ocellated Turkey of Central America; but although few in number, yet considering what they have done for man's comfort and welfare, and as the source from which has been derived the domesticated race introduced into many lands, our magnificent birds may be considered with perfect propriety the most important members of the Phasianidæ throughout the World.

SUBFAMILY MELEAGRINÆ.

THIS division of the great family of the Phasianidæ includes only the Wild Turkeys of the New World. By some ornithologists these birds are deemed worthy of being considered a distinct family—Meleagridæ, but it does not appear that any particular advantage is gained by so elevating them, or that these birds are any more entitled to such a rank than many other species of Phasianidæ which have always been enrolled in subfamilies. The Turkeys are no more characteristic and distinctive than are the Pea-fowl, Tragopans, Crossoptilons, and many others that might be mentioned, and are naturally a portion of the one great family, containing the spurred, beautifully plumaged fowl comprising the Phasianidæ. The Turkeys are of course very distinct from Partridges and Grouse, and are properly placed in a different family, their many and peculiar characters separating them widely from the members of Tetraoninæ, with which indeed, beside a dress of feathers, they have little in common. Beside the two North American species and the two races, only one other species is known, the wonderfully plumaged Ocellated Turkey of certain portions of Central America, which in its gorgeous metallic hues is not surpassed in brilliancy by any other known bird.

As game birds in the highest sense, affording sport in the field, as well as food to countless people, the Turkeys are among the most important members to the human race of the feathered tribes.

For over one hundred years the specific name of *gallopavo*, Linn. has been applied to the common Wild Turkey of North America (the *Meleagris sylvestris novæ angliæ*, of Ray, Av. 51); and by that name, even among non-scientific persons, it is pretty generally known. The fact as to what particular bird Linnæus had before him, and which became his type when he wrote the description in the Systema Naturæ,—whether one of the domesticated race descended from the Mexican Turkey, or an example of the common North American species,— cannot now be established with any degree of certainty, and whatever change is made in the nomenclature of the Wild Turkeys can have no solid foundation to rest upon. But in regard to this point, a spirit of unrest is abroad, and a new shuffle of the synonomy is attempted, and among some ornithologists our northern bird is called *americana*, a name without a description, given by Bartram (Travels, 1791, p. 290), and by others *sylvestris* (Viell. N. Dict. d'Hist. Nat., 1817, vol. ix. p. 447), a name taken from Ray, *l. c.*, while the long employed and familiar term of *gallopavo* is made to do service for the White-rumped Mexican bird. It is of little consequence by what name a species is called, provided it is one accepted generally by ornithologists; and a change should not be made unless it can be conclusively proved that the name in use has been incorrectly adopted. It is not apparent that in this instance it can be proved that this has been the case, and the question then becomes one of individual opinion when a change is agitated.

In a popular work, such as this book pretends to be, the principal effort should be to furnish its readers with the latest information on the subject of which it treats, and to give the reasons, when possible, why any changes are made, especially in the cases of long-accepted and well-known terms. The author may or may not be in sympathy with the attempted innovations, and, as in the present case, may find it as impossible to prove them erroneous as do its advocates to establish their correctness, but as his chief object is to portray the species contained in this volume, so that they may be recognized by his readers when met with elsewhere, and also be possessed of the same names, he has followed this new departure, even though it may not be permanent.

If a change must be made from long-established and harmonious custom, there is no question as to which names the species of Turkeys must bear, according to the A. O. U. code.

The common Wild Turkey must take the name of *sylvestris*, Viell., and not of *americana*, Bartram, which is a *nomen nudum*, and the Mexican Turkey must be known hereafter as *gallopavo*, Linn., although that naturalist may never have seen the bird.

Under the guise, therefore, of these new appellations according to the very latest ideas, the Turkeys have been arranged in the following key:

GENUS MELEAGRIS

(Greek, μελεαγρις, *meleagris*, a guinea fowl).

Meleagris, Linn. Syst. Nat. ed., 10, vol. i., 1758, p. 156. Type, *M. gallopavo*, Linn.

Head and upper part of neck, bare, carunculated, the male with a dewlap considerably developed and an erectile process at base of bill. Tarsus scutellated broadly before and behind, armed with a spur in the male. Plumage compact, metallic, the North American species with a tuft of hairlike feathers depending from the breast.

One species and three subspecies inhabit North America. One of the subspecies, *M. s. elliott*, on account of the conspicuously different markings of the female, quite unlike any other known form of turkeys, might properly be assigned a full specific rank. These noble birds are too well known to make it necessary to go into any details regarding them, beyond the accounts given in the various articles in the body of this book. From the Mexican and not from the North American bird came our stock of domestic Turkeys, and nearly all the latter exhibit in their light rumps and upper tail-coverts the proof of their descent. The so-called Bronze Turkey of the farm-yard has, however, a large percentage of the blood of the wild Northern bird in his veins.

KEY TO THE SPECIES.

A. Tail tipped with deep rusty, upper tail-coverts tipped with chestnut.

a. Bars on primaries reaching the shafts.	WILD TURKEY. *M. sylvestris.*
b. Bars on primaries not reaching the shafts.	FLORIDA WILD TURKEY. *M. s. osceola.*

B. Tail and upper coverts tipped with ochraceous buff.

ELLIOT'S RIO GRANDE TURKEY. *M. s. ellioti.*

C. Tail and upper coverts tipped with white.

MEXICAN WILD TURKEY. *M. gallopavo.*

INDEX.

ADAK ISLAND, 163
Agattu Island, 151
Akun Island, 159
Akutan Island, 159
Alaska, 88, 89, 90, 94, 95, 106, 108, 126, 151, 153, 167
Alaska, Northwestern, 100
Alaskan Coast, 151
Aleutian Chain, 156, 159, 161, 163, 165
Aleutian Islands, 158
Amchitka Island, 161
America, 38, 142
American Museum of Natural History, 107
Anderson River, 123, 151
Anthony, A. W., 47, 48, 59
Arctic America, 153
    "   Ocean, 142
    "   Regions, 104, 124, 147, 151, 206
Arctic Sea, 199, 204
Argus Mountain, 44, 46
Arizona, Southern, 39, 49, 52
    "   Territory of, 20, 38, 49, 62, 67, 69, 72, 89, 93, 182, 185
Artemisia, 136
Asia, 208
Assiniboia, 136, 141
Astoria, 41
Atka Island, 161
Attu Island, 161, 165

BAD LANDS, 132
Baird, S. F., 150
Barboquivari Range, 38
Barren Grounds, 151
Behring Sea, 151
    "   Straits, 88
Belt Range, 106
Bendire, Capt. C., 42, 44, 47, 58, 59, 67
Bishop, Mr., 102
Bob White, 19, 20, 21, 22, 25, 27, 32, 33, 35, 36, 37, 38, 39, 41, 67, 77, 110, 192, 194, 195
Bob White, Florida, 32
    "   Masked, 38, 194
    "   Texan, 35, 36, 194
Bob Whites, 193
Boisé City, 20
    "   River, 20
Bonasa, 200
    "   umbellus, 80, 87, 201
    "   umbellus sabini, 83, 201
    "   umbellus togata, 87, 201
    "   umbellus umbelloides, 88, 201
Brazos River, 180, 181
Brewster, William, 118
British America, 123, 125, 171
    "   Columbia, 57, 81, 84, 88, 106, 108, 126, 136, 141, 167
British Columbia, Northern, 83, 87

British North America, 98, 99
British Possessions, 100
"   Provinces, 74, 147
Brown, Herbert, 38

CALIFORNIA, 20, 30, 41, 42, 44, 46, 55, 60, 67, 81, 83, 90, 94, 95, 126, 136, 141
California Coast Region, 57
"   Lower, 44, 47, 48, 58
"   Southern, 44
Callipepla, 193, 195, 197
"   squamata, 52, 196
"   squamata castanei-gastra, 54, 196
Cambridge, 118
Canachites, 200, 202
"   canadensis, 104, 202, 203
Canachites franklini, 108, 202, 203
Canada, 84, 142, 167, 172
"   Dominion of, 84, 87
"   Southern, 80
Cape St. Lucas, 55, 57, 68
Capercailzie, 136, 198
Cascade Mountains, 170
"   Range, 84, 167
Central America, 208, 209
Centrocercus, 200, 205
"   urophasianus, 141
Chilcat Peninsula, 142
Coast Range, 41, 81, 83, 94, 97, 106
Cock of the Plains, 90, 136, 200, 205
Cock of the Woods, 136
Colinus ridgwayi, 39, 194
"   strenua, 188
"   virginianus, 30, 34, 194

Colinus virginianus floridanus, 33, 194
Colinus virginianus texanus, 36, 187
Colorado, 20, 88, 90, 129, 134, 141, 167, 170
Colorado Desert, 62
"   River, 49
Columbia, 41
Connecticut, 117
Coues, Dr. Elliott, 67
Crossoptilons, 209
Cumberland Gulf, 154
Crytonyx, 193, 197
"   montezuma, 72

DAKOTA, 110
"   South, 19, 30
"   Southwestern, 90, 93
"   Western, 88
Dakotas, The, 74, 80, 115, 132, 136, 141
Death Valley, 58
Dendragapus, 200, 201
"   obscurus, 93, 97, 98, 99, 202
Dendragapus obscurus fuligi-nosus, 97, 202
Dendragapus obscurus richard-soni, 99, 202

EASTERN HEMISPHERE, 186, 192, 199, 201
England, 184
Europe, 184
Evermann, Professor, 165

FANNIN COUNTY, TEXAS, 49
Fisher, Dr., 44
Florida, 19, 30, 32, 33, 34, 172, 176, 179

Forest and Stream, 102
Fort Brown, 120
" Chimo, 150
" Simpson, 124
" Union, 62
" Whipple, 69
France, 184
Franklin Bay, 151

GEORGIA, 74
" Northern, 80
Great Salt Lake, Valley of the, 20
Great Slave Lake, 123
Greenland, 151, 153, 154
Grouse, 74, 77, 79, 82, 84, 85, 86, 88, 89, 94, 98, 100, 104, 123, 126, 127, 128, 130, 189, 191, 199, 209 .
Grouse, Blue, 89, 90
" Canada, 100, 101, 106, 108, 202, 203
Grouse, Canadian, 85, 201
" Canadian Ruffed, 74, 84, 194
Grouse, Columbian Short-tailed, 124, 126, 131, 205
Grouse, Dusky, 90, 91, 94, 97, 99, 103, 200, 202
Grouse, Fool, 92
" Franklin's, 106, 107, 108, 202, 203
Grouse, Gray, 90
" Oregon, 81
" Pine, 90
" Pinnated, 115, 117, 118, 120, 127, 128, 129, 134, . 140
Grouse, Pintail, 126
" Prairie, 192
" Richardson's, 98, 202

Grouse, Ruffed, 74, 77, 79, 81, 82, 84, 88, 103, 199, 200, 201
Grouse, Ruffed Gray, 88, 201
" Sage, 136, 137, 139, 140
" Sabine's, 81, 82, 201
" Sharp-tailed, 123, 124, 128, 129, 134, 136, 140, 200, 204
Grouse, Sharp-tailed Prairie, 126, 129, 132, 205
Grouse, Spike-tail, 126
" Spruce, 199, 200, 202
" Sooty, 94, 98, 157, 202
" Willow, 142, 149, 150, 151, 152, 154, 155, 157, 161, 167
Gila Monster, 65
" River, 72
Gilroy, 20
Guadalajara, 36
Gulf States, 172, 176

HAWKS, 79
Heath Hen, 111, 117, 204
Hempstead Plains, 117
Hen, Fool, 92
Huachuca Mountains, 38
Hudson Bay, 123, 124, 151
" Strait, 164
Humbert River, 150

IDAHO, 20, 30, 84, 88, 98, 167
" Northern, 87, 106
" Southeastern, 99
" Southern, 80, 90, 93
" Western, 97
Illinois, 129, 134
India, 208
Indiana, 110
Indian Territory, 19, 115, 120, 172
Inyo County, California, 44
Iowa, 110

KADIAK ISLAND, 100, 104
Kansas, 19, 110, 115, 120
    "   Southwestern, 120
Kentucky, 110
Kentville, 103
Klamath Valley, 58
Kyska Island, 163

LABRADOR, NORTHERN, 154
    "   Southern, 151, 153, 154
Lagopus, 200, 205
    "   evermanni, 165, 207
    "   lagopus, 147, 150, 206
    "   lagopus alleni, 206
    "   leucurus, 171, 207
    "   rupestris, 153, 206
    "   rupestris atkensis, 161, 207
Lagopus, rupestris nelsoni, 207
    "   rupestris reinhardi, 200, 207
Lagopus rupestris townsendi, 161, 163, 207
Lagopus rupestris welchi, 157, 207
Lagopus Scoticus, 206
Lake Superior, 124
Liard River, 99, 171
Lockhart River, 123
Long Island, 117, 119
Lophophorus, 208
Lophortyx, 192, 193, 196
    "   californicus, 57, 60, 197
Lophortyx californicus vallicola, 60, 197
Lophortyx gambeli, 67, 197
Louisiana, 19, 110, 115, 122

MACFARLANE, MR., 123

MacFarlane River, 151
Maine, 19, 30, 84, 104, 172
Manitoba, 110, 115
Martha's Vineyard, 111, 117, 119, 129, 203
Massachusetts, 74, 80, 117, 119
Meleagridæ, 209
Meleagrinæ, 183, 209
Meleagris, 211
    "   gallopavo, 185, 211, 212
Meleagris sylvestris, 176, 179, 181, 212
Meleagris sylvestris ellioti, 181, 211, 212
Meleagris sylvestris novæ-angliæ, 210
Meleagris sylvestris oceola, 179, 212
Mexico, 36, 38, 39, 180, 182, 184, 199
Mexico, Eastern, 53, 180, 181
    "   Northern, 49
    "   Northeastern, 54, 181
    "   Northwestern, 62, 67, 69
Mexico, Table-land of, 72
    "   Valley of, 50
Minnesota, State of, 74, 104
Michigan, State of, 74, 115, 172,
Mississippi, State of, 80, 172
    "   River, 19, 30
    "   Valley of the, 110, 115
Missouri, 19, 30, 110
Mogallon Mountains, 49
Mojave River, 58
Montana, 88, 98, 106, 126, 128, 129, 134, 167
Montana, Northwest, 108
Monterey, 57

Montezuma, 185
Mount Kearsage, 44
" Magruder, 46

NEBRASKA, 141
Nevada, State of, 46, 58, 60, 67, 90, 97, 126, 141
New Caledonia, 84, 87
" England, 22, 87, 104, 147
Newfoundland, 147, 149, 150, 157
New Hampshire, State of, 19
New Jersey, State of, 117, 119
" Mexico, Territory of, 19, 30, 49, 52, 62, 67, 69, 70, 72, 89, 90, 93, 129, 134, 136, 141, 167, 171, 182, 204
New Mexico, Northern, 62
" World, 142, 184, 185, 191, 199, 206, 209
New York, Northern, 87
" State of, 19, 104, 142, 150
North America, 151, 160, 191, 192, 199, 202, 203, 204, 206, 208, 209, 210, 211, 212
Norton Sound, 88
Nova Scotia, 103
Nuevo Leon, 36

ODONTOPHORINÆ, 191, 192
Ohio, State of, 74, 115, 172
Old World, 191, 205, 208
Ontario, 115, 172
" Southern, 19, 30
Oregon, 20, 30, 41, 42, 55, 57, 58, 60, 84, 87, 106, 108, 128, 136, 141
Oregon, Eastern, 46
Oreortyx, 193, 194
" picta, 194
" pictus, 42, 46, 195

Oreortyx, pictus confinis, 48, 195
" pictus plumiferus, 46, 195
Ortyx, massena, 197
" montezuma, 197
" squamatus, 195
Owls, 79, 82

PACIFIC, 30, 81, 126
" Coast, 42, 81, 100, 106, 142
Panamint Mountains, 46, 60
Partridge, 19, 69, 71, 74
" American, 191, 192, 209
Partridge, California, 55, 56, 59, 62, 71, 196, 197
Partridge, Chestnut-bellied, Scaled, 53, 196
Partridge, Birch, 74
" Black, 69, 100
" Black-bellied, 69
" Blue, 49, 52, 71, 196
" Gambel's, 51, 55, 58, 62, 64, 66, 70, 71, 195, 196, 197
Partridge, Massena, 69, 70, 71, 193
Partridge, Mountain, 41, 44, 45, 157, 195
Partridge, Plumed, 44, 45, 195
" San Pedro, 47, 195
" Scaled, 49, 50, 52, 53, 195, 196
Partridge, Spruce, 100, 101, 104, 106, 107
Partridge, Valley, 58, 107
" White Top-knot, 49
Partridges, 189; 201
" Helmeted, 193
" North American, 192

Partridges, Plumed, 193
   "   Scaled, 193, 197
Pea-fowl, 209
Pediœcetes, 200, 204
    "   phasianellus, 124, 204
Pediœcetes phasianellus cam-
   pestris, 134, 205
Pediœcetes phasianellus co-
   lumbianus, 128, 205
Pennsylvania, Eastern, 119
    "   State of, 117,172, 176
Perdicinæ, 191
Phasianidæ, 183, 208, 209
Phasianus, 208
Pheasant, 74
Pine Hen, 89, 90
Plomoso, 38
Polyplectrum, 208
Prairie Chicken, 110, 111, 114, 115, 126, 127, 129
Prairie Chicken, The Northern, 120
Prairie Hen, 110, 114, 203
   "   " Attwater's, 122, 204
   "   " Lesser, 120, 204
Prairie Hens, 202, 203, 204
Ptarmigan, 183, 184, 200
    "   Allen's, 149, 206
    "   Evermann's, 165, 207
Ptarmigan, Nelson's, 159, 207
Ptarmigan, Newfoundland, 157
    "   Reinhardt's, 154, 207
Ptarmigan, Rock, 151, 155, 161, 206
Ptarmigan, Townsend's, 163, 207

Ptarmigan, Turner's, 161, 207
    "   Welch's, 157, 207
    "   Willow, 151, 152, 206
Ptarmigan, white-tailed, 167, 207
Puget Sound, 20, 55

QUAIL, 19, 23, 24, 25, 27, 28, 33, 35, 36, 62, 63
Quail, Black, 69
   "   Black-bellied, 69
   "   Cactus, 49
   "   Crested, 50
   "   Florida, 33, 34
   "   Fool, 69, 70, 198
   "   Gambel's, 39, 62
   "   Masked, 38
   "   Mountain, 169
   "   Snow, 169
   "   Texan, 37, 40
   "   Valley, 58, 62
   "   White, 169
   "   White-crested, 49
   "   White Topknot, 49
Quails, 191
Quickiock Falls, 153

RIDGWAY, R., 73
Rio Grande, Foothills of the, 53
Rio Grande, Lower Valley of the, 54
Rio Grande, Valley of the, 35, 53, 69
Rocky Mountains, 93, 94, 98, 99, 100, 104, 108, 123, 126, 134
Rocky Mountain Region, 88
Rocky Mountains, Eastern, 128

SAGE COCK, 137, 199, 205

Sage Hen, 138
San Antonio, 69, 120
San Bernardino County, California, 62, 67
San Francisco, 41, 42, 46
San Pedro Mountains, 47, 48
Seattle, 41
Sennett, G. B, 53, 180
Sierra Nevada Mountains, 44, 46, 58, 94
Silver City, 72
Sitka, 90, 142, 147
Snake River, 20
Sonora, 38, 39
Sonoita Creek, 38
    "   Valley, 38
St. Augustine, 177
St. John's River, 177
St. Lawrence, Gulf of, 153
Staked Plains, 35

TAMAULIPAS, 36
Taos, 69, 167
Tetrao californicus, 196
    "   canadensis, 202
    "   cupido, 203
    "   lagopus, 205
    "   obscurus, 201
    "   phasianellus, 204
    "   umbellus, 200
    "   urophasianus, 205
    "   virginianus, 193
Tetraonidæ, 191, 192
Tetraoninæ, 150, 189, 199, 209
Texas, 19, 35, 49, 53, 54, 110, 115, 120, 122, 172, 176
Texas, Eastern, 30
    "   Gulf Coast of, 122
    "   Western, 36, 49, 52, 62, 67, 69, 72, 120, 182, 185

Townsend, Mr., 163
Tragopans, 209
Tucson, 38
Turkey, Bronze, 212
    "   Eastern wild, 181
    "   Elliot's Rio Grande, 180, 212
Turkey, Florida wild, 177, 178, 212
Turkey, Mexican, 182, 185, 210, 211, 212
Turkey, Northern Wild, 179
    "   ocellated, 208, 209
    "   wild, 172, 173, 175, 176, 180, 182, 208, 212
Turkeys, wild, 183, 208, 209, 210
Turner, L. M., 154
Tympanuchus, 200, 203, 204
    "   americanus, 115, 119, 203
Tympanuchus, attwateri, 122, 204
Tympanuchus, cupido, 119, 204
    "   pallidicinctus, 120, 122, 204

UNITED STATES, 19, 38, 49, 51. 69, 87, 90, 106, 111, 123, 124, 167, 172
United States, Eastern, 19, 30, 80, 85, 88, 180
United States, Middle, 19, 111, 117
United States, Northern, 19, 33, 39, 180
United States, Northwestern, 126
United States, Southern, 22, 36, 74, 180, 181, 191
United States, Western, 19, 101, 117, 162, 166, 167, 171

Utah, 20, 30, 58, 90, 141
   "   Southeastern, 62, 67

VALLADORES, 47
Vancouver Island, 42, 81
Vermont, State of, 19
Virginia, State of, 20, 74, 119

WASHINGTON, State of, 30, 41, 42, 55, 57, 84, 87, 106, 108, 126, 128, 136, 141
Western Hemisphere, 191, 192
West Indies Islands, 184

White-belly, 132
White Mountains, 49
Willamette Valley, 41, 58
Wilmot Horton River, 151
Wisconsin, State of, 74, 129, 134, 172, 176
Wyoming, Northern, 99
   "   State of, 90, 98, 126, 128, 167

YUKON River, 89
   "   Valley of the, 88

ZEREGA, L. A., 150

COLOR CHART

❧

The Chart at the end of this volume will greatly assist readers to identify the various colors mentioned in this work.

www.ingramcontent.com/pod-product-compliance
Lightning Source LLC
Chambersburg PA
CBHW031401270325
41929CB00010BA/1274